ANN PHILLIPS

The Oak King
and the
Ash Queen

*for Newnham Croft School
from Ann Phillips*

OXFORD UNIVERSITY PRESS 1984

Oxford Toronto Melbourne

Oxford University Press, Walton Street, Oxford OX2 6DP

Oxford London
New York Toronto Melbourne Auckland
Kuala Lumpur Singapore Hong Kong Tokyo
Delhi Bombay Calcutta Madras Karachi
Nairobi Dar es Salaam Cape Town

and associated companies in
Beirut Berlin Ibadan Mexico City Nicosia

Oxford is a trade mark of Oxford University Press

© Ann Phillips 1984
First published 1984

All rights reserved. No part of this publication may be reproduced,
stored in a retrieval system, or transmitted, in any form or by any means,
electronic, mechanical, photocopying, recording, or otherwise, without the
prior permission of Oxford University Press

This book is sold subject to the condition that it shall not, by way of
trade or otherwise, be lent, resold, hired or otherwise circulated
without the publisher's prior consent in any form of binding or cover
other than that in which it is published and without a similar condition
including this condition being imposed on the subsequent purchaser

British Library Cataloguing in Publication Data

Phillips, Ann
The Oak King and the Ash Queen
I. Title
823'.914[J]   PZ7
ISBN 0–19–271495–3

Typeset by Oxford Publishing Services, Oxford
Printed in Great Britain by Biddles Ltd., Guildford

Summer

1

There was Aidan Sturgess, commonly called Dan, asleep under an oak tree in the middle of the Forest in the hottest part of the day. He appeared quite an ordinary boy — not a graceful sleeper, being a sprawling bundle of arms and legs; and damply pink with the heat. The person who was standing over him appeared anything but ordinary. For a start, he was about 200 centimetres high; then, he was extremely brown-skinned and was wearing a belted, sleeveless tunic which ended just above his knees. His short hair was reddish and curly and he looked about thirty-five.

The tall man only looked at Dan for a moment. Then he stood astride Dan's body and, leaning his left hand flat against the trunk of the oak, laid his right hand on Dan's head.

Dan woke up with a start and jerked into a sitting position. The man stepped back and nodded to him. Dan stared.

'What is it?' he said. 'What do you want?'

'Your service,' said the man.

Dan didn't like the sound of that and changed the subject quickly.

'Who are you, then?' he asked.

'You have three questions, starting from now,' said the stranger. 'You are allowed three questions each time we meet. But not, of course, that one. And nothing to do with names.'

'I don't mind telling you my name,' said Dan.

'I already know it, thank you,' said the stranger politely. 'You're often about in the Forest. Ask your three questions, if you're going to.'

Dan thought briefly, and asked his first. 'Why are you dressed like that?' Privately, he thought the stranger must be a member of a film company remaking *Robin Hood* or some other film with medieval peasants in it.

1

'I'm always dressed like this,' said the stranger. 'Except for the great occasions, when I dress up a bit. Next question?'

Not an actor then, thought Dan. Maybe a gypsy?

'Where are the rest of your people?' he asked.

'All around,' said the stranger. 'I can see two of them from where I'm standing.'

'I can't see anyone,' said Dan, diverted.

'So I imagine,' said the man. 'You aren't educated in looking. You can have one more question.'

'How old are you?' asked Dan, and held his breath.

'I can't give you a very precise answer,' said the man. 'Something over 170 years, but less than 175. Does that satisfy you?'

'Yes, thanks,' said Dan. So, he thought, it's what I was afraid of. He is an alien.

After a tiny pause, Dan stopped looking at the alien's long, narrow, bare feet. He looked at his ears instead, but they weren't pointed.

'You said you wanted a service,' he said. 'Do you want to be taken to a scientist or somebody? — A leader?' he added, patiently, as the alien looked baffled.

'You haven't understood,' said the alien. 'I'm in command myself here, and I have all the knowledge I need. I am the king.'

'Oh,' said Dan. There seemed nothing else to say, as he had used up his three questions.

'Now as to the service,' went on the king. 'It's perfectly simple, and any child — so long as he's human — could undertake it. But we're too public here to explain it. Woods have ears. Come with me to my own place.'

Dan scrambled rapidly to his feet. He had no intention of going anywhere with this alien. 'Never speak to strange aliens' flashed, ridiculously, through his mind.

'I'm sorry,' he said. 'I'm not going.'

'You most certainly are,' said the alien calmly. 'You've no power to refuse.'

2

For answer, Dan took to his heels. He realized that on the flat the tall king could outrun him, but he hoped that by dodging among trees he could make use of his smaller size to escape.

He had gone about five steps, over tree roots and moss, when he heard a thud behind him, as if a foot had stamped heavily on the ground, and the alien's voice said, 'Hold!' Immediately Dan had the horrible sensation of sinking into the ground. He wondered for a wild moment whether the earth was opening to swallow him up; but he only sank up to his ankles. When his ankle-bones were covered, the earth seemed to harden round him, and his feet were held as fast as if he had been set in concrete.

'You see,' said the king agreeably, behind him. 'I hold the dominion of earth. Hence I can control movement.'

Dan had lost his temper. 'You talk like some wishy-washy sci-fi rubbish,' he said as he struggled, straining knee- and hip-joints, to free his feet. 'I don't believe in the dominion of earth. It sounds like Tolkien and that sort of stuff.' His voice expressed contempt for fairy-tales, folklore, Enid Blyton and all associated gnomery.

'Don't scoff at the earth,' said the king sharply. 'Or what will bury you when you're dead?'

'I shall be cremated,' puffed Dan, still struggling.

'Ah, very likely,' said the king. 'We were coming to that.' He put a hand on Dan's shoulder: it was cool through Dan's shirt, and hard.

'Loose,' he said, and stamped lightly. At once the ground around Dan's feet seemed to slacken and melt, and he stepped free. But he couldn't pull away from the king's hand.

'Now we'll go to my hall,' the king said pleasantly. 'But first, a ceremony.' Still holding Dan, he recited seriously:

'Out iron, in wood.
Guard the trees' good.'

Dan felt a curious sensation, as if all the fillings in his teeth (not very many, fortunately) moved and jarred. At the same time, his treasured watch fell off his wrist, and the buckles slipped to the ground from his sandals and the elastic belt of his shorts.

'Hey,' he said. 'My watch!'

The king scooped a scattering of dead oak leaves over it with his foot.

'It will be safe enough,' he said. 'No metal is permitted in my hall — or where I and my people are. Step out of those shoes, or they'll fall off you as we go.'

Dan did, and tied the ends of his belt in a knot. He felt secretly glad there was no zip in his shorts.

'What about my teeth?' he said, testing them with his tongue. 'They feel funny.'

'That metal,' said the king, 'is protected by the surrounding bone. I've heard that when people have more metal than tooth, it disengages itself.'

Dan gritted his own disturbed teeth at the thought.

'And now we go,' said the king, still affable.

They went. Dan made a few more attempts on the way to shake off the king's hand, but it only settled more firmly each time he tried. It weighed light, but its grip was unyielding.

They went a winding way, deeper into the Forest, not following any visible path but twisting among the trees and undergrowth. The king moved with the lightness and balance of a dancer and no brambles seemed to touch him. Dan, unused to going barefoot, walked warily. Sometimes he stubbed a toe on a tree root; sometimes a thorny creeper scratched at his bare ankles. He was glad that the previous few weeks had been dry ones, and that there was more dust underfoot than mud. Watching his feet as he had to, he noticed a curious thing. Whereas in the dusty places his feet left bare, man-Fridayish prints, the king's much larger feet left no mark at all. Nor did they break loose twigs and fallen branches which they touched.

Another slightly strange thing he observed was that birds

and woodland animals didn't seem afraid of them. Birds several times whirred down towards the king with a chirp or a call, and once a pheasant ran out of a bush and came up almost to their feet — Dan was afraid he might fall over it. Rabbits, shrews and voles were much more easily seen than Dan thought usual; and once he was sure he caught a glimpse of a fox behind a tangle of brambles.

They went in silence, and they went — it seemed to Dan — fast. He lost his breath and felt that he must be steaming with the heat, though the king's hand on his shoulder felt as cool as it had done at the start. When Dan was about ready to drop, the king pulled him suddenly to a halt.

'Here we are,' he said, and Dan looked around.

They had reached a high point in the Forest where rocks outcropped among the trees; trees grew more sparsely and ferns and foxgloves appeared between them, and thin grass.

'Now meet the two of my people who have been travelling with us,' said the king. 'Beech! Apple!'

While Dan was puzzling over these names (he knew a boy called Beach; but 'Apple'?) two more people dressed like the king stepped out of the trees. They nodded civilly to Dan.

'Beech,' said the taller of the two; he was taller, even, than the king, and looked older. He had dark, smooth hair, grey-sprinkled, and green eyes, and was a very dignified figure.

'Apple,' said the shorter — hardly more than 180 centimetres, Dan estimated. He looked about eighteen, was rosy-cheeked beneath his tan and had a shock of light brown hair.

'Good afternoon,' said Dan, and the two replied together, 'Welcome to the kingdom!'

The king shifted his grip to Dan's wrist, and before Dan had time to register the distinguishing marks of the place he had tugged him under a low-hanging branch, through an opening between two rocks and into a dark tunnel. Dan found it frightening. His feet slid on bare rock and dust, his free hand, snatching at the side, caught uselessly at earth and tree roots. The tunnel was only a few metres long, but it went sharply down; then light grew and Dan, towed behind the king, skidded out into a huge, underground room. It struck him as being a room, not a cave, because it was quite light. Daylight filtered in several places between roots and trails of fern and shafted down to a floor covered with a matting made out of something coarse and hairy, like a network of root fibres. Also, it was furnished. There was a simple trestle-table surrounded by plain, wooden benches; there was also a sideboard holding an array of wooden beakers and bowls. The walls appeared to be beaten earth, and all around were large-headed pegs on which hung or were propped a variety of weapons — spears, arrows and bows.

Four or five people, dressed like the king, stood up from where they were sitting on tree-stump stools against the wall, and bowed to him.

The king let go of Dan. 'My hall,' he said with satisfaction. 'This is the seat of the Oak King.'

Dan flopped down, exhausted, on one of the benches.

The king made a signal and the other men there, including Beech and Apple, all seated themselves on stumps. One person, however, whom Dan only caught a glimpse of, slipped away and seemed to disappear into the shadows at the entrance. He looked no more than a boy, perhaps only Dan's age, and was strikingly pale.

'And now,' said the king smoothly to Dan, 'the service you are to do for me. I want fire, boy. Fire.'

'Fire!' said Dan, violently surprised. 'Do you mean firearms? Guns?'

'Of course not,' said the king, looking forbidding. 'Those are iron and steel. I couldn't touch them. No, I want simply fire: the fire you use to light your kindling. All men have it: it's in some sense their prerogative. And what damage they do with it! One your size can burn a forest down.'

'Matches,' said Dan. 'But you don't need matches. Provided you have dry sticks, you can make fire by friction. Even I can do that. These loose sticks on the floor would do.'

6

'Yes, if I had time on my hands,' said the king. 'When I need fire for a special reason, as I do now, I need fire I can make fast. Matches, you call them? Have you got them?'

'No,' said Dan. 'My father won't let me carry them about.'

'A wise father,' said the king. 'Go and fetch them.'

'No, look here, honestly,' said Dan. 'I can't! I don't know what you want them for, or who you are, or anything. How do I know you won't burn the Forest down yourself?'

'And a wise son,' said the king. 'I'll answer you. Today is Midsummer Day. You know that, of course.'

'Of course,' said Dan. He had only known it was Saturday.

'And tonight the people of the trees light their midsummer fires,' said the king. 'I, the Oak King, share the rule over the trees with the Ash Queen; and we share the dominion of fire. Each of us should bring one-half of the fire-cross to the ceremony and we should light the fire together. But my half of the fire-cross is missing; I can't do my part.'

'And so you want matches,' Dan said thoughtfully. 'Why me?'

'You're here, and it's convenient,' said the king. 'There was a girl, too, but you were nearer to my tree.'

'My sister,' said Dan, leaping up. 'I'd forgotten Daisy. She'll be looking for me everywhere.'

'On the contrary,' said the king. 'She is, like you, a prisoner. A prisoner of the queen.'

— 2 —

It was a fine time for Dan to be remembering his sister. She had been having, if anything, a worse time than he had.

Diana Sturgess, commonly called Daisy, was Dan's twin. Like many pairs of twins, they quarrelled a good deal more often than they agreed. Their quarrel that day had been one of the most stupid. It should have been a glorious day — an all-day picnic in the Forest near their home, on a dry, bright, burning summer Saturday. But what should they fall out over but a simple thing like where to eat their midday sandwiches. Dan wanted to go up to a high point, where there was a wide view from an outcrop of rocks; Daisy wanted to go down to the river that ran through much of the woodland. So they split up the food (badly, as it turned out: as well as half the sandwiches Dan had all the cake, and Daisy had both apples), and separated — the thing they had promised their parents never to do.

Daisy didn't miss Dan. Their house was so close to the edge of the Forest that they were very much at home among the trees; and although the Forest was big enough to get lost in several times over, Daisy felt secretly sure that she could always find her way out alone.

The area which the local people called 'the Forest' or 'Hart-wood' was in fact huge, and it wasn't all woodland. It would take a good walker the best part of a summer day to go round its boundaries; and inside those boundaries were several distinct areas of woodland (including the Low Woods and a hilly part known as the High Forest) some boggy bits, some open, scrubby places, some fields used as pasture, two farms, and half of the Sturgess's village, St-John-in-the-Wood. Red deer, a small herd and seldom seen, roamed as they liked; and so at times did half-wild ponies from the nearest hills.

Once on her own, Daisy went straight to her favourite place, where there was a clearing which gave a level stretch of grassland on either side of the river. Elders and willows stood around and made it a secluded place. The bank was not steep here, and she pushed her way through the flowers of purple loosestrife, wild yellow iris and meadowsweet to a smooth part where there was room to lie, and a higher bit of the bank free of forget-me-not and watercress. Her sandals came off and her legs up to the knee went into the water, and she sat in a happy daze. In the same daze, and unconscious of time (she had left her watch at home) she ate her meal, including both apples, and had a drink of river-water from her cupped hands. Then she settled back comfortably on the grassy patch behind and relapsed into a (mainly horsy) dream. The rubber band holding her longish hair at the back of her head stuck into her head-bones, so she took it off and draped the hair on either side across her shoulders. The sun was hot on her face and life was altogether delightful.

Something, suddenly, jerked her painfully to her feet. It was as if somebody had taken hold of her hair in both hands and pulled her up — but she could see nobody. Immediately afterwards a gust of wind of immense power took hold of her and whirled her away from the water and up to the edge of the trees, and brought her up smack against the trunk of an ash tree. She felt what seemed to be a hand on her forehead. When it was drawn away she found herself looking at a tall and very upright young woman, who was standing right beside her.

'Did you do that?' asked Daisy, frightened into anger.

'Of course; and I have a right to. I am the queen,' said the woman.

'You don't look anything like her,' snapped Daisy. She had never actually seen the Queen, but her photographs were always in the paper.

'Dismiss your preconceptions,' said the queen, grandly but quite politely. 'I am the Ash Queen, and share the rule of the Forest with the Oak King. These are some of my people.'

Daisy realized with a shock that there was a group of women and girls standing around them. Like the queen, they all wore short, belted tunics of green or greenish-brown, and were barefoot; most had long hair, but some wore it in plaits or buns. Their dress had the appearance of a uniform. Daisy wondered if they were some eccentric ramblers' club on a back-to-nature walk. They were all by human standards extremely tall.

'I didn't see anyone here a minute ago,' she said. 'Were you hiding?'

'No, but invisible to you,' said the queen. 'You could see none of us until I touched you and my tree at the same time.'

'I don't believe it,' said Daisy.

'Then look at us well, and try to begin,' said the queen. 'Since you're going to spend some time with us —'

'No I'm not,' said Daisy promptly. She was beginning to find the whole experience creepy.

'Don't waste your breath on defiance,' said the queen. 'If you mean to go, try it.'

Daisy did try it; but the moment she attempted to walk away from the tree the queen raised her hand, and a huge, quick puff of wind flung Daisy back. This time she banged her head against the tree.

'I hold the dominion of air,' said the queen, smiling.

'But what *are* you?' asked Daisy, really alarmed. 'Are you — fairies?' She hesitated over the word. It seemed an odd one to apply to such tall people.

'Yes, if you like the word,' said the queen. 'It's not one I'd use myself. We are the people of the trees. But this isn't the place to talk about secret things: come along.'

She caught Daisy's hand and said, as the king had done over Dan:

'Out iron, in wood.
Guard the trees' good.'

Daisy had no watch and no sandals on, but a metal grip fell out of her hair and she felt the same twinges in her filled teeth as Dan had done in his.

At once a gale seemed to spring up around them. All of them — queen, Daisy and followers — were blown, feet hardly touching the ground, into the depths of the trees; up and down wooded slopes, through thickets and clearings; until they landed in an abrupt dead calm in a place where Daisy had never been, where a dark, silent pool lay among close-crowding trees. It was a small pool and branches hung

10

low over it and made it black with shadows. The water was completely still; the few leaves floating on its surface did not even rotate. The feel of the place was deeply sinister, and Daisy was struck rigid with fright.

'One of my gateways,' said the queen, sweeping the long, pale hair out of her eyes. 'We go in.'

'No!' exclaimed Daisy. No power on heaven or earth should take her into that water.

The queen fixed her with a compelling stare. 'Don't be stupid,' she said. 'I also hold the dominion of water.' She laughed, and pulling Daisy after her ran along a thick branch which projected over the water at ground level; and with a wide leap plunged into the middle of the pool.

Although the water was warm, the shock of it knocked all the sense out of Daisy. She retained no clear idea of how deep the pool was — only that she seemed to be dragged downwards for a long time; or how they got out of it, although she was aware that the queen began after a while to tow her not downwards but sideways. Her feet grated on mud and pebbles, and something more solid; and suddenly her head was out of water and she was being hauled up a shingly slope into a low, underground chamber.

Even as water poured off her, and she gasped and coughed it up and rubbed it out of her eyes, Daisy couldn't help noticing that the queen, and the followers now emerging around her, were untouched by damp. They were not out of breath and their hair and clothes were not even disarranged. The indignity of being dragged through a hideous, black pond seemed much worse to Daisy in that its effects were not shared.

'You'd better not just stand dripping,' said the queen. 'Movement will dry you.' She took Daisy by the hand again and ran her at high speed through several wet and slippery vaults of rock of varying sizes, some with small, shallow pools covering their floors and some with stalagmites and stalactites forming. Most were dark, with a little light coming from rock-clefts here and there. Daisy slid and sploshed and was heartily relieved when they came out into a dry-floored, beautiful cavern, the size of a small church. One end of it was a natural arch, through which they entered; on either side of them were walls of stone, sloping outward from the high peak of the roof. The fourth side of the cave was open to the air — but not just to air; it was covered by a curtain of falling water, and the noise of water filled the place.

'I know where we are,' Daisy exclaimed, distracted from her wet and miserable state. 'We're behind the waterfall — the one that's called the Veil.'

'The *Queen's* Veil,' the queen corrected. 'Sit down, all the company. It's a time to talk.'

There were natural shelves of rock running around the walls, with clumps of ferns growing from crevices nearest to the light. Near the waterfall the shelves were wet with spray. Daisy felt she was wet enough already and made for a dark, dry niche, but the queen pulled her out and seated her on a tree-trunk stool in the centre, and herself sat on another.

'And now,' said the queen to Daisy, 'you may as well tell me the whole story. The king has taken your brother. What is it he's got that the king wants?'

Daisy was totally disconcerted. 'I don't know,' she said. 'What king? Will Dan be all right? He hadn't got anything except his sandwiches.'

'The Oak King,' said the queen impatiently. 'I told you. Your brother has either got something or knows something. You may as well understand that I shall never let you go until I'm told what it is. So think. Hard. And quickly.'

Daisy couldn't think of anything. She sat huddled, still damp, and feeling more and more dejected. At first there was no sound but the noise of the waterfall; then the queen's people began to talk softly amongst themselves. The queen sat silent.

'Well?' she said at last. 'Can you think of anything useful; or will you stay here all night?'

Daisy was shaking her head helplessly when somebody else came into the room. He entered, dramatically, through the waterfall; but there was no water on him when he stood clear in the cave. He was a slight, pallid creature who looked as if he might be in his early teens, with a cloud of fluffy, very pale hair, and eyes — slightly protruding — the colour of ripe gooseberries.

'Is it you, Ash Queen?' he said. 'My eyes are dazzled by the light.' He shaded them with his hand. The queen stepped forward and touched his shoulder.

'I'm here,' she said. 'What are you doing in my hall, Mistletoe? Have you come from the king?'

'He didn't send me,' said Mistletoe. He had a very soft, light-toned voice. 'But I've been there. He's got a human prisoner.'

'So I heard,' said the queen. 'But why? This girl is the human boy's sister. She says she doesn't understand.'

'It's altogether strange,' Mistletoe said. 'The king says he wants fire; he expects the boy to get it.'

'Fire!' said the queen, startled. 'But it's my half of the fire-cross that's gone, and not his. What does he mean?'

'Perhaps he means to make sure you can't repair your loss, by capturing the human people's fire for himself,' suggested Mistletoe.

'Do you understand any better now, girl?' the queen said to Daisy.

'Not a bit,' said Daisy. 'Is it matches he wants? I could easily get him some.'

'You'll get him nothing,' said the queen sharply. 'You'll get these matches and you'll bring them straight to me. It's I who need them. My half of the fire-cross has been lost since the spring festival, and I need it tonight. Mistletoe, go back to the king's hall; see what else you can discover. Girl, come over here. I must talk to you secretly.'

Mistletoe bowed and slid away again into the mist of the waterfall. The queen pulled Daisy close to the fall, so that the water's noise made their talk private, and put a hand on her shoulder. It was uncomfortably rigid.

'This is some plot of the king's,' she said. 'I don't know what he intends; but certainly my part of the fire-cross has gone, and without it I shall be ashamed tonight. You must choose your allegiance. If you choose me, get these matches and bring them here.'

Daisy found she couldn't look away from Ash's grey-green eyes. 'I promise,' she said. 'I'll help you. I don't see why the king should plot against you. Shall I come straight back?'

'Come at midnight,' said the queen. 'I shall send for you. Tell me your name — then there can be no mistake.'

'Daisy,' said Daisy, still not taking her eyes off the queen.

'Is that your common name? Or your real one?' the queen asked.

Daisy looked baffled.

'My people call me "queen" or "lady", and my common name is Ash,' said the queen. 'But I have a real name too, one that isn't known — Samara.' After she'd said it (she pronounced it to rhyme with camera) the queen stopped abruptly and pressed her lips together. Daisy guessed that she hadn't meant to mention the secret name at all.

'Mine's Diana,' she said. 'Sturgess is my common name.' It sounded very common indeed.

'I shall call you,' said the queen. 'Go off now on your quest.'

'But how?' asked Daisy, nervous. 'I'm not going back through that pond.'

'You can go down the Queen's Veil,' said Ash. 'Alder!' A dark woman, much older than the queen, came quietly forward and bowed, her penetrating, black eyes on Daisy.

'Take the girl down the Queen's Veil,' Ash ordered.

Daisy felt that descending the waterfall would be just as bad as going through the pool: but it wasn't. Alder guided her to the side of the cave, and out through the floating spray on to the rocks. Mercifully the cave turned out to be near the

14

foot of the fall, and Alder, with a firm hand on Daisy's elbow, steered her down the short and slippery climb.

'Do you know where you are?' she asked, when they stood at the base of the tossing, twisting, cascading tumble of water, in a drift of cold droplets.

'Yes, thanks,' said Daisy briefly. 'My shoes are further down the river, and the lunch-bag. I'll get them first.'

She set off at a headlong run along the bank, happy beyond words to be out in the air again. And alone.

—— 3 ——

'Look, you must let me go,' said Dan to the king. 'I ought to have stayed with my sister — we told our family we'd always keep together in the Forest. I feel responsible for her.'

'I don't see why,' said the king. 'The two of you seem much of an age, and equally incompetent. Do you swear to bring me fire?'

'No,' said Dan sulkily. 'It seems a pretty weird story — the missing fire-cross, and all that. I'm not convinced.'

The king frowned ferociously, and made a movement of impatience; then cleared his throat with a growl, and said, 'Forget fire. I shall persuade you, but I won't do it by ill-treatment. Nor do I mean you should starve. We'll eat and drink now, and you can rest.'

The people in the hall jumped up, looking keen. Apple went outside and called, and several more followed him in. They all went to the sideboard and filled, each one for himself, small wooden bowls from the larger ones there. Some took their food from a single bowl, others mixed the contents of two or three. Wooden pitchers of water were put on the table, and the men brought their bowls back to the table, poured water into them, stirred the mixture with wooden spoons and ate it with enjoyment. Dan, deeply interested,

15

looked to see what it was. Unmistakably, they were eating earth. Blackish or brownish, watered-down, sloppy, gritty, uneatable earth.

Dan turned his horrified face to the king. The king's bowl had just been brought to him by a boy called Bramble, and he was stirring it with gusto. Seeing Dan's disgust, he laughed.

'Well, what do you expect us to eat?' he said. 'We're Trees, you know. Don't worry, we'll bring you something you can manage. Apple and Hazel are fetching yours. Bramble, bring him leafy dew to drink; nothing but the best for guests.'

From the bottom of the sideboard, Apple and Hazel brought Dan some very withered looking apples (last year's), and hazel-nuts still in their shells. Dan didn't fancy the apples, and had no crackers for the nuts. But a slim, young person also brought him wild cherries — underripe and very sharp, but refreshing; and Bramble poured him, from a special pitcher, a drink of the most delicious clean water. Dan drank a lot.

While they ate, the tree-people laughed and talked with animation, and finally started singing. Dan liked the sound of their songs and believed he recognized a bit, here and there, from some of the folk-songs he and Daisy had sung at school. One song he was sure was a version of 'The Keeper', and ended like it, 'Among the leaves so green-oh'.

During the singing, the king beckoned Dan to his side. Dan sat on a stump stool and felt nervous.

'Have you had second thoughts about bringing fire?' asked the king.

'How can I decide?' said Dan, trying a little cunning. 'I don't know anything. About you, for example. You say you are trees, but you look like people — very tall people. Why?'

'You had your three questions,' said the king, with a laugh. 'But never mind; I'll give you another three. We *are* Trees. Each tree has its own person — you might say, its soul; and each kind of tree sends one chosen person to serve on the king's council and in the king's band of warriors.'

'But you look like men,' persisted Dan.

'Of course,' said Oak. 'How could we look like trees — with no hands for action, no feet for movement, no mouths to talk? The chosen tree-people must take some other form than that of trees, in order to come to the king's council.'

'Well!' said Dan. 'You could have been birds. Or animals — woodland animals, foxes or badgers or deer. Why men?'

'We once,' said the king, 'shared a religion with men. You might say, a culture. We first took the form of men in order to share in ritual and celebration. We found it convenient, and we kept to it.'

'A religion!' said Dan. 'You mean, the Druids?' He had vague recollections of hearing that the Druids had been involved with trees. Oak trees, was it? Mistletoe?

'Oh, before that,' said the king. 'In the time of the primeval forests. The first religion of all. The rising of the sun, the turning of the year, the growing of things; and their death and burial. You know it — everybody does. It's our religion still, of course. Even some of you still believe in it.'

Dan's ideas of religion were shadowy, but this didn't sound like anything he had ever heard of.

'And is fire part of it?' he asked.

'That's four questions,' began Oak.

'The first two were the same one,' said Dan. 'You'd better tell me, if you want my help.'

'Yes, of course, fire,' said the king. 'All four dominions are part of it. Earth, water, air, fire. Earth is mine; air and water are the queen's. Fire we share.'

'If she has water and air, the queen must be stronger than you,' said Dan. He had no more questions, but he still wanted to know.

'You don't know that,' said the king. 'Nobody knows that.' He looked, suddenly, sad and savage, and muttered what sounded like 'the elms, the elms!'

'So some of the dominions are more powerful than others,' said Dan.

17

'You might say so,' said the king. 'You'll see, of course, why we share fire. It is essential and appalling; a terror and a need. The end and the beginning. Neither of us could possess it alone.'

'I've made up my mind,' said Dan abruptly. 'I won't get it for you. Now that I know.'

The king stretched and smiled. 'And I know *you*,' he said. 'You've eaten and drunk here. You are a witness. You will get fire, and come when I call. At midnight, if not before.'

'No, I won't,' said Dan. 'And now I've got to go outside.' He had drunk a lot of water and his anguished glance around the hall showed no doorway which might have led to even primitive mod. cons. He was embarrassed, but the king was not.

'You animals!' said the king. 'How useful you are! Choose an oak tree.'

He waved a hand to the entrance door, and Dan shot off in relief and ran full pelt up the tunnel.

He did choose an oak tree; and afterwards, feeling better, he looked doubtfully back towards the way into the hall. Was he expected to go back? No one had followed him.

'If he wants you, he'll fetch you. He can, you know,' said a voice from the shade of a dense little holly tree. The pale, thin boy who had left the hall just after Dan arrived, stood there. 'Did you eat and drink in there?' he asked.

'Yes — cherries and something called leafy dew,' said Dan.

The tree boy drew in his breath with a hiss. 'Then he's got you,' he said. 'You've eaten his food and drunk his sacred wine.'

'It was water,' said Dan.

'All the same,' insisted the skinny boy, 'you're in his clutches. You'll go when he calls.'

'I shan't,' said Dan cheerfully. He sensed freedom and felt, happily, his own man again. 'I'm a human being, not some sort of a bush. And who are you? Are you one of them? You're not much taller than I am.'

18

'Mistletoe,' said the pale boy. 'One of them, but at the same time not. I don't belong. No ground-roots, you know.'

'Can you tell me where I left my sandals and my watch?' said Dan.

'I should guess it was at the King's Oak,' said Mistletoe. 'A huge oak tree, was it? On its own? Follow along, then.'

Dan was willing to follow, but Mistletoe was a stumbling and uncertain guide.

'Take my arm,' he said, after a step or two. 'I don't see well in this bright light. My eyes are better in the winter, and at night.'

They came, after what seemed a much shorter journey than the outward one, to the tree where Dan had met the king. Dan saw his sandals at once; he scuffled among the dry oak leaves, and found his watch and the buckle off his belt. His sandal buckles — so tiny — seemed to have gone for good.

Mistletoe tensed and stepped away when Dan stood up, triumphantly showing his watch and the buckle.

'The Death,' he muttered through his teeth. 'Don't come too near.'

'Oh, come on,' said Dan. 'I know it's a rule with you — but honestly, you couldn't cut down a tree with a watch or a bit of a belt-buckle. What's the danger?'

'It's death and destruction,' Mistletoe said emphatically. 'Man's weapon. If you carry metal, I'm the only one of the Trees who'll come near you; and even I don't like it much, I'll admit.'

'All right,' said Dan. 'I know more or less where I am now; you can leave me to find my way alone. But you might just guess, if you can, where my sister has got to.'

'I'll try,' said Mistletoe. 'Listen, and keep utterly still.'

In the quiet they heard the scratchings and scrabblings of small animal life, minute leaf-noises, small birds' conversation, and suddenly, far off, a jay's harsh shriek.

'That's where she is — where the jay called,' said Mistletoe. 'By the river, where the ford once was.'

19

'How can you tell?' asked Dan.

'The jay was warning of a large animal nearby, and I haven't heard deer or ponies around,' said Mistletoe. 'Or any people except you two. That's how we know most things we know: birds tell us.'

'I thought that was a joke,' Dan said.

'Go straight away, if you're going,' said Mistletoe as the jay cried again. 'She's moving away from the waterside.'

Dan took his sandals in his hand, jerked out his thanks, and set off at a run.

He didn't meet Daisy on the river path. Daisy was not going home, she was looking for him. As he came to a standstill, having temporarily lost his sense of direction, he heard in the distance feet moving at a jog — a sound of urgency. He shouted, and got a shout back — 'Here, Dan, here!' They came together running, wild with eagerness to share their news. For several minutes there was a noisy chaos of talking-at-once. Dan finally managed to shout the louder of the two.

'I know, I know — the queen got you. But listen — a chap called Mistletoe says I'm in the king's clutches and I'll have to take him fire. I don't mean to.'

'No, don't,' Daisy interrupted. 'The queen says it's a plot. It's her fire that's lost, not the king's.'

'But that's weird,' said Dan, arrested. 'The king sounded perfectly genuine. His half of the fire-cross was lost and he needs it for a ceremony tonight — lighting a midsummer fire, if I got it right.'

'So did the queen sound genuine,' said Daisy. 'Her half of the fire-cross has been lost since spring. She says that without it — or matches as a substitute — she'll be ashamed tonight.'

'How can both halves be lost?' said Dan. 'It seems ridiculous.'

'Dirty work,' said Daisy with relish. 'And that Mistletoe — did you say he helped you? He came to the queen's hall and told her what was going on in the king's. He's a spy.'

20

'He did say he didn't belong anywhere,' Dan recollected. 'And, Daisy, we shouldn't be discussing it all in among the trees, like this. The king said woods have ears.'

'That's not the only thing — what's the time?' Daisy asked urgently.

'Five fifteen; no hurry. We needn't be home till six,' said Dan.

'We've just got time before the shop shuts,' said Daisy. 'Come on — my purse is in the lunch-bag, and I can buy for both of us.'

'Buy what?' asked Dan.

'Matches, of course,' said Daisy. 'It doesn't seem right to take Mum's for this, does it?'

'You mean you're going back to the queen, tonight, and taking her her precious fire?' said Dan. 'Daisy, you must be mad! These people are dangerous, powerful and dangerous. I'm not going within a mile of that Oak King again.'

'I promised to help,' said Daisy. 'What's so dangerous? I *like* the queen. This is positively the most exciting thing that's happened to me all my life.'

Both as set as fighting stags, the two confronted each other.

'We'll see what Dad says,' growled Dan.

'Now *you're* being mad,' said Daisy. 'We can't tell Dad! We may be safe among the tree-people, but Dad wouldn't be. They won't do anything to us, because we're children and not a threat to them. They'd drop a tree on Dad as soon as he got involved.'

Dan tried to argue, but Daisy refused to talk any more. 'Woods have ears,' she insisted. 'I'm off to the shop.'

At the pace she set, Dan — still running barefoot — had a job to follow her. They were into the village and at the shop by five forty-five — it was open until six. Daisy bought Swan matches, feeling nothing but the best would do for the queen; Dan (just in case) bought safety matches, wondering bitterly where the safety was. They also bought ices to cool themselves after their furious run, and strolled home licking.

21

'You're right,' said Dan to Daisy, when they got to the gate of Fosters, their house. 'Look!'

'I'm looking,' said Daisy. 'What's the tree that overhangs the house on the Forest side, with a big branch close to the roof and its twigs almost in at Margie's and my windows? An ash. And what's the tree that overhangs the garage, with Dad's trusty steed inside? An oak. They've got us surrounded; all of us. Mum and Dad and Margie — they'd better not know.'

'I still don't mean to help the king,' said Dan uncomfortably. 'I don't want anything to do with the tree-people. You may feel safe with them, but I don't.'

'What makes you think you'll have any choice?' Daisy asked, sucking the sticky traces of the ice off her hands. 'They said they'd call us.'

'I wonder what they mean,' said Dan uneasily.

'You've only to wait,' Daisy said.

—— 4 ——

The children had expected it to be desperately difficult to contain themselves and not to talk at home about their afternoon's adventures. In the event, nothing could have been easier. They burst into the kitchen to find no tea laid, and no anxious parents wondering if they had survived a day in the Forest unscathed. Only Margaret, their seventeen-year-old sister, was at home; and she was lying on a pile of cushions on the sitting-room floor listening to a classical guitar record and smiling faintly to herself.

'Oh, are you back?' she said vaguely to the twins. 'Had a good day? Get your own tea, if you want any; I've had mine.'

'Where are Mum and Dad?' asked Daisy.

'Away for the night — they told you,' said Margaret. 'In London; going to the National Theatre and staying with

Doug.' (Douglas was the eldest of the 'children' of the family, with a new job in London and a flat of his own.)

'So they did,' said Daisy. 'The famous wedding anniversary, no less. When did you have your tea, Margie?'

'Oh, ages ago,' said Margaret. 'Jamie was here. I made a cake; there's some left.'

'It's no good talking to her,' said Dan loudly to Daisy. 'She's not really hearing us. It's my belief she's in love again.'

'Not again — still,' said Daisy. 'It was Jamie yesterday.'

'It's to our advantage,' said Dan when they were safely in the kitchen. 'Marg won't notice a thing if the tree-people come tonight. She's like a zombie when she's in love. Who's cooking? If I am, it's eggs. Tortured, tinned or umlaut?'

'Umlaut,' said Daisy. 'I'll do salad.' She didn't like either scrambled or boiled eggs much.

It was a good meal, but a silent one. The twins ate with the concentration of the young and hungry; and in the centre of the table, occupying their thoughts, stood two boxes of matches.

By the time they went to bed the moon was up, its brightness combining with the last remaining daylight; garden flowers and shrubs and the Forest beyond stood motionless, colourless and two-dimensional in the flat brilliance. Dan, who wasn't afraid of the dark but found moonlight spooky, drew his curtains, shut his window and pulled a sheet over his head. He intended to sleep through the entire night's proceedings if he got a chance. Daisy set her alarm for midnight and put the clock under her pillow; she left her curtains and her window wide open, and thoughtfully put beside her bed a skirt with an elasticated waist, a T-shirt and a pair of plimsolls with elastic tops. The matches were under her pillow with the clock.

Neither Dan nor Daisy expected to sleep; they both went to sleep immediately. This was just as well: it was not very long before they were called.

Daisy woke first. She was startled awake by the heavy,

23

thudding beating of wings just over the house, and a rattle like a gust of wind in the ash boughs just outside her room. Twigs — or was it fingers? — rapped at the open casement and a soft voice said, 'Diana!' She was out of bed and at the window in one movement. Balanced in the branches of the tree was one of the queen's people, a slim girl with very light, shining eyes and a drift of pale yellow hair; and on the grass beneath, neck arched up towards her, was a magnificent swan.

'You are called,' whispered the girl. 'Follow the swan to the river. You are called!'

'I'll just get dressed,' began Daisy.

'No time for that,' said the girl. 'Follow the swan!' She dropped out of the branches of the tree and was gone among the bushes.

Swan. Matches. Daisy grabbed them, de-alarmed her clock, and went downstairs barefoot and in her long, pink night-dress, her loose hair in tangles. Margaret, whose bedroom was next door to hers, never heard a sound and didn't even twitch in her sleep.

Dan woke, however. Dan woke to his own calling. No voice, no bird, no person. He woke with an intense, passion-ate, unbearable desire to be in the Forest. To be there at once, to be there without going. It never occurred to Dan to get dressed. He didn't even remember his matches: but the over-powering wish to get to the Forest included an overpowering wish to put the matchbox in his pyjama pocket. He did it without noticing the action and got downstairs without notic-ing the treads.

He and Daisy met in the hall, where Daisy was fumbling for the Yale lock. They didn't speak to each other, but Dan steadied the door as Daisy pulled it shut behind them; it made only the smallest click. Daisy slid the key under an empty milk-bottle and looked around for the swan: it was now among the first of the trees, beyond their garden gate.

Fosters stood alone, the very last house in the village; the only house beyond the church of St John, and at the end of

24

the made-up road. Past its gate, the road turned into a track and the track into a forest ride. There was no one about to see two children in night-clothes slip into the trees.

Once among the shadows of the wood, the children stopped.

'I'm not going with you, am I?' said Dan.

'Who are you following?' said Daisy. 'I'm following the swan.'

'I'm following my feelings,' said Dan. 'I'm doing what I want to do. I saw Hazel ahead in the trees: perhaps he's going with me. I'm off.'

And he *was* off, running fast and steadily up the ride. Daisy saw a tree-person, coming out of the darkness, set off after Dan; this being's footsteps made no noise.

At the same moment the swan took off and rose, its wing-beats thundering, into the bright, blank sky.

'That's hopeless,' thought Daisy. 'How can I follow it if it flies?' But as before, she had the sensation of being lifted off the ground by whirling air and carried by a moving belt of it. She kept her eyes on the swan and her feet ran under her; but they weren't touching ground. After a minute she simply let them dangle, loose at the knees. She was between the trees, not above them; but the course set by the swan, directly above her now, kept her always clear of branches. She felt a cold excitement. This was flying. This would have been the most thrilling experience of her life, if she had been quite sure it was her life.

Strangely, although Daisy's looking was all concentrated on the swan, she knew approximately where she was and was conscious of approaching the river. The swan began to descend, its wing-beats slurring. Daisy's progress through the trees slowed too. As the swan came lower, her field of vision dropped; she became aware of a group of people — the queen, surely, and some of her women? — standing — where? They appeared to be standing in the river: but not in it, on it, somehow suspended on the water's surface.

25

The swan touched down with a long, loud, braking splash. Daisy realized, in a moment's panic, that she was coming down in the river too. She landed close behind the swan, drawing her breath in preparation for a shocking sinking through the water. But she didn't sink. The water felt cool against the soles of her feet, and held her up, rocking her lightly; the ripples of the swan's wake broke gently over her toes.

'Come on!' called the queen, who was several metres away. 'I hold the dominion of water! You can walk on it.'

Daisy tried a tentative step and found that the water buoyed up her moving weight. Saints do this, she thought, and angels fly; I've done both . . . and she bowed to the queen as she arrived in front of her. It seemed appropriate.

'Fire,' said the queen. 'Where is it?' Daisy realized the matchbox was all this time clasped in her hand. She gave it to the queen who examined box and matches with interest.

'It bears my mark — the swan,' she said. 'A royal bird, symbol of the domain of water.'

'Only by chance,' said Daisy.

'Oh — chance!' said the queen scornfully. She dismissed chance. 'Listen now — listen! The king is coming.'

All the tree-people on the river, and Daisy, stood silent: they heard a distant singing in the Forest. They strained their eyes, and all at once they saw in the moonlight a procession of figures come out from the trees, dancing as they came and singing softly. The queen whispered to Daisy, 'Is your brother there? Is it he who's walking beside the king?'

'Yes,' said Daisy. 'He can't do country dancing. Only the disco kind.'

At the river's edge the king bowed and called to the queen, 'May we tread your water, lady? May we enter the domain?'

'Enter, tread and dance,' said Ash.

The king and his people danced their way on to the river, and the queen and hers danced to meet them; they joined on the water in a longways dance rather like 'Sir Roger de Coverley', but more stately. Daisy got hold of Dan and

26

showed him what to do. Dan had always managed to be involved in football practices when they had country dancing at school. A little wooden pipe and a small drum made music for the dancing.

Daisy noticed, now they were at close quarters, that the tree-people were wearing their party clothes — long, floating robes of green and grey and brown and black and silver. Ash wore a ring of smooth wood set with a huge pearl, and one ear-ring, which glinted blue; Oak wore a pendant on a leather string — it appeared to be a flat, greenish pebble pierced with a round hole.

The water-dancing went on for some time. Daisy loved it. She found the water enjoyably springy, like downland turf or the grassy tops of cliffs. Even Dan decided there might be something in dancing, when it involved rivers and cool, sweet air and the middle of the night. At one point Ash danced alone, as she danced taking off and playing with her pearl ring which she threw to one Tree after another, who caught it and threw it back with, at each catch, joyful shouts and clapping.

'What is it about the ring?' Dan whispered to his neighbour, a Tree whose name he didn't yet know. 'Is it special?'

The Tree turned a startled face to him. 'The symbol of water,' he said. 'The badge of her power. It's crucial.'

'Oh,' said Dan. 'So the king wears a pebble; and the queen's ear-ring is what — butterfly-wing?'

He got no answer and deduced that he was right.

'What's happening now?' demanded Daisy. She was standing between Dan and the Tree who had come to call her (who was, she had discovered, Silver Birch). 'Who is dancing now with the queen?'

A skinny young girl, with a pale green robe and long red-brown hair, had caught Ash's ring in the dance; instead of throwing it back to the queen she was twirling and spinning in a lively dance of her own, now and then making as if to throw the ring to Ash but catching it back at the last minute. Her whole manner was light-hearted and teasing, but Silver Birch seemed shocked by her performance.

'She shouldn't be here,' she muttered, more to herself than to Daisy. 'It's Larch. They should drive her out.'

'Oh? What's she doing wrong?' Daisy asked. But before Silver Birch could answer her the queen had, with a single gesture and with a lowering look, summoned two of her people, who now advanced towards Larch at a run. Larch did a final, challenging jump and flung the ring back to Ash; then — still dancing — backed away laughing from the two women Ash had sent towards her.

'She's not one of us, that's all. She's not even invited here,' said Silver Birch. 'Haven't you heard of the winter people?' She stamped, snapped her fingers and ran to join in the general dance, which had now become a noisy promenade around the queen.

Larch's backwards dance took her to where the children were standing, a little separate from the dancers. Daisy caught at her sleeve as she came level with them.

'You can come and stand with us,' she said. 'I don't understand why they're throwing you out, and it doesn't seem fair at all.'

Larch smiled and shrugged, as if she dismissed Daisy's views of fair and unfair. 'I take a risk when I come here,' she said. 'And it's high time I was off. Good-night.' She sketched a quick bow to them and they lost sight of her among the dark tree-shadows.

Finally, the tree-people invited the twins to do a human beings' dance and stood around to watch.

'Oh heck,' said Dan feelingly under his breath. 'I'm not up to solos. What can we do?'

'Pretend it's a disco,' said Daisy. 'Give it all you've got.' They hurled themselves into what in the Sturgess family was known as the grizzlies' minuet. The tree-people watched with startled respect.

When the twins stopped for a moment Daisy heard one Tree say to another, 'It's a war-dance.'

28

'How do you know?' asked the second.

'Oh, by the threatening gestures. It's quite plain,' said the first.

'Enough of dancing,' said Ash when the children finished. ('Follow that,' said Dan to Daisy between puffs for breath.) 'The water is to be fetched for the New Year.'

The fetching of the water involved, besides Ash herself, three of her people — Willow, Alder and Aspen. These four led the whole party in a processional dance to the very ash tree which had knocked the wind out of Daisy when Daisy first met the queen. Under the tree were four pitchers of water, which the four leaders picked up. The Trees all laughed and cheered, and the four used part of the water to splash and sprinkle all those around them, who competed enthusiastically to get wet.

'Only they don't stay wet,' said Daisy to Dan, shaking drops out of her hair. 'It's all right for them.'

The Trees now took up a new song, and chanted it high-spiritedly as the procession went to the Queen's Veil waterfall; up this the Trees danced, and into the queen's hall; out again and down the waterfall.

The children did not attempt this. As they stood watching, Mistletoe left the dance and came to stand between them.

'Trees don't get out of breath,' said Dan. 'I couldn't dance up a waterfall, let alone singing.'

'We breathe mainly through our skins,' said Mistletoe. 'Throat breath is all for speech and music.'

'I half know that song,' said Daisy. 'It's very like one our school choir sings. But I couldn't get all the words.'

Mistletoe took up what the tree-people were singing:

> 'Here we bring new water
>   from the well so clear
> For to worship God with
>   this happy New Year.
> Sing leafy dew, sing leafy dew,

> the water and the wine,
> The heaven's bright gold showers,
> the becks and pools that shine.'

There was more of it, and when it finished the Trees began it all over again.

'It's not quite the same as our words, but almost,' Dan said. 'Why are they singing it now? It's not New Year.'

'Of course it is,' said Mistletoe impatiently. 'It's the summer solstice. The days get shorter now; the year begins to wane. You can celebrate New Year now as much as at the winter solstice.'

'Your years are only six months long,' said Dan.

'Or you might say they overlap,' said Mistletoe.

'And what's all the water-carrying for?' asked Daisy.

'This is the water festival,' said Mistletoe. 'Water at midsummer; earth in autumn; fire at midwinter; air in spring. Times and seasons. You people used to understand and celebrate with us.'

'But June's a dry time of year,' objected Daisy.

'Of course. That's why,' said Mistletoe. 'The four kinds of water are taken up and carried to the queen's and king's halls; and we light the summer fire.'

'What four kinds of water?' asked Dan. 'Tell us quick; they're coming down the waterfall.'

'River water, rainwater, spring water and leafy dew,' said Mistletoe.

'So they were in the four pitchers,' said Daisy. 'But what's leafy dew?'

'Your brother drank it. The wine of the trees,' said Mistletoe. 'Water that drips from leaf to leaf of a tree and so down — filtered through leaves, tasting of greenness. A sacred drink.'

'Delicious,' remembered Dan. 'They're moving again, Mistletoe. Is it to the king's hall now?'

'It is, and the dance gets faster,' said Mistletoe. 'You'll

30

never keep up. We'll cut that stage out and I'll take you direct to the fire-place — to the central stone.'

The fire-place was a wide clearing deep in the heart of the High Forest; the children had never seen it before. Moonlight through branches dappled and hatched it. In its centre lay a flat, oblong stone, still bearing the ashes of old fires. When the tree-people came dancing into the clearing they were all carrying sticks and branches they had picked up on their way; they threw these on to the central stone as they danced around it, and stood silent in a wide ring as the king and queen met at the stone. Daisy looked around for Larch, but couldn't see her.

'It is the fire-time,' said the queen. 'Let each of us take a fire-branch and let the cross be made whole.'

There was dead silence among the Trees.

'My arm of the fire-cross is not with me, queen,' said the king. 'I bring a brand.' He struck a match and tossed it into the heap of dry wood; a few sticks caught.

'What sort of trick is this?' said the queen, drawing in a sharp breath. 'My arm of the fire-cross has been lost since the spring Change. I too bring a brand.' She struck a Swan match and it too went into the kindling; bright flames began to creep up and a cheerful crackling sounded.

'You try my patience,' said the king. 'I don't play tricks. My fire-branch was lost at the Change, as well as yours.'

'You try my strength,' said the queen. 'Can I believe you?'

'My word — ' began the king.

'— is yourself,' the queen cut in. 'And my word is mine. But I'm not mad, and our two words together add up to madness.'

'It needn't be madness,' said the king. 'There may be some reason here which is true reason. Take it that neither you nor I has fire. I have only earth, you have air and water. Without fire which keeps the balance, whose strength is the greater?'

'Is it time, then?' said the queen. 'My elms have died in millions. Is it time?'

31

'It is time,' said the king.

'Time for what?' Dan muttered urgently to Mistletoe. 'They sound terribly serious.'

'For a trial of strength,' said Mistletoe. 'The king and the queen have declared war.'

As if to illustrate his words, Oak and Ash clasped their right hands like arm-wrestlers, tensed and pulled themselves together as arm-wrestlers do; and after a moment's equal struggle, pushed themselves apart. They dropped hands, both smiling with a cold gleam.

'War!' said Dan, alarmed and excited. 'Are we in it?'

'Oh yes,' said Daisy, 'bound to be. But we're on different sides.'

—— 5 ——

'Our ceremonies must be cut off short,' said the king coolly to the queen.

'Very little remains to be done, in any case,' said the queen. 'Only the torchlight dance and procession, and the burning of the dead. All that can be left until after the war.'

'Certainly,' said the king. 'How many days do you need to prepare?'

'Give us three,' said the queen — with something of the eagerness of a person ticking off the days before a holiday. 'Three days from now our bows will be strung and our spears sharp for you.'

'It all seems very gentlemanly,' Dan whispered to Mistletoe. 'Wouldn't they do better to take each other by surprise?'

'Wars between kings and queens are courteous wars,' said Mistletoe. 'Who fight yours?'

'Professionals, mainly,' said Dan. 'Full-time soldiers. Kings and queens are kept somewhere safe.'

'Degenerate,' said Mistletoe. 'I wouldn't trust war-men to run a proper war.'

Dan was drawing breath to argue, but the king spoke directly to him.

'Your presence is required,' he said. 'You fight on my side.'

'But I can't!' said Dan, torn between longing and cold feet. 'School doesn't finish for weeks — not till July the eighteenth.'

'And you?' said the queen to Daisy. 'Is your school the same?'

'We go together. It's a mixed school,' said Daisy. 'We have to go. It's the law.'

'The law!' said the king and queen to each other. They took that as final.

'When your school is done, you come to me,' said the queen to Daisy. 'As a witness, and to fight.'

'But I don't — I've never —' began Daisy. 'Girls don't fight.'

The king and his men laughed heartily; Ash glittered with anger, her eyes bright as ice in the moonbeams.

'You speak an outrage,' she said to Daisy. 'What world is it where females don't fight! It must be a world devised by males, where they can triumph unopposed.'

'— and foully dull it must be,' finished the king. 'Who wants an unarmed victory?'

'You have until your school-time ends,' said Ash to Daisy. 'And then you will return, proficient — note this — proficient in the spear and the bow. Or it will go badly for you. Return incompetent, and you will in all likelihood die in the battle.'

Dan rushed to the defence of Daisy — of both of them, in fact. 'We don't use spears and bows,' he said. 'Not since the sixteenth century or so. People have fought with guns since then. Only archery-nuts use bows.'

'Then become one!' exclaimed Oak, now as angry as Ash was. 'You have a month, or near it. Return an archery-nut or return to your death. And return you will: you will be called, and this time you can expect a different calling.'

33

'And now go,' added the queen. She and the king stood side by side, stiff with offended dignity.

'Shall I take them?' asked Mistletoe. 'They'll be lost in the Forest if they go alone; no human beings know their way to or from our gathering-floor.'

'Yes, go with them,' said the king. 'Your eyes will be better than theirs in this light. Get them away from here.' He and Ash turned away, and Mistletoe gripped an arm of each child and hustled the two of them into the shadows.

The sense of lightness and excitement which had buoyed up Daisy and Dan now left them. They felt tired, frightened and depressed and their bare feet were cold. The moon was going down; the night was losing its warmth. Daisy would have burst into tears on even slight provocation, and to tell the truth, so would Dan.

There was no breath left for talking, as Mistletoe set a good pace and there was a long way to go. Nobody said a word until Mistletoe finally stopped, in the beech ride leading towards Fosters gate.

'Your home,' he said. 'May I give you some advice, before I go?'

'About spears and bows?' said Dan wearily.

'About not disparaging what is sacred to others,' said Mistletoe. 'Longbow and spear have served the balance for an age; and to slight the prowess of a warrior-queen is to speak like an idiot.'

'Well, it was true,' said Daisy sulkily. 'Girls don't fight in our world.'

'Poor creatures!' said Mistletoe with scorn. 'Your world must lack balance. And heart.'

'Look — what are we to do?' said Dan. 'We've only got titchy little bows and arrows, that we made ourselves when we were six. I'm not even sure they still exist — Dad may have burnt them when he turned out the garage, any time in the last six years. We haven't played with them since we were seven.'

34

'Played!' exclaimed Mistletoe. 'There you go again!'

'Don't be cross,' said Daisy. 'What *are* we to do, Mistletoe?'

'Well!' said Mistletoe. He smiled importantly. 'If you were just to send a message, nicely-worded, to Ash and Oak to say that you had no weapons of your own, something might be done.'

'But I still don't think I want to fight,' moaned Daisy. 'War's a horrible thing, anyway; and cruel.'

'You weren't offered a choice, that I heard,' said Mistletoe. 'The question isn't whether or not you fight, but whether you get killed fighting. You're in no position yet to judge the wars of the Trees.'

'Then please say to the king, Mistletoe,' said Dan, 'Aidan Sturgess will serve him as a bowman but has no bow. Will that do?'

'Bowman and spearman,' said Mistletoe. 'He expects both.'

'And the same to the queen,' said Daisy gloomily.

'From Diana,' said Mistletoe. 'Good sense. Good morning, Aidan and Diana!' Without a sound, he was gone among the trees.

'He's right, it *is* morning,' said Daisy. 'Listen — the dawn chorus!' It was hardly a chorus yet, but a bird or two just beginning to speak.

'Let's go to bed, Daise,' said Dan. 'We've been up all night.'

If Margaret wondered in the morning about earthy footprints in the hall, and a dry leaf or two on the stairs, she never mentioned it. Neither did she comment on the fact that the twins were still asleep when she went to church at nearly eleven, and had only just finished a colossal breakfast when she got back at after twelve.

'Get dressed,' was all she said. 'If Mum and Dad find you still in dressing-gowns when they get back, they may never dare to stay away again!'

The Sturgess parents were back in time to eat a late lunch, which Margaret, Daisy and Dan had got ready between them.

35

They had had a very good time, and as they did most of the talking the twins' silence went unnoticed. Margaret's didn't, but Mr and Mrs Sturgess already knew about Jamie and were unsurprised.

(Mrs Sturgess did have a few words to say about Dan's having lost not one, but both sandal buckles; but his promise to take the sandals to the repair-shop himself after school made some amends. 'Released with a caution,' Daisy whispered to him.)

By common consent, Daisy and Dan said nothing to each other about trees for the rest of the day. Dan went down into the village and found his friends Terry and Jenk; Terry had a motor bike and Jenk was always now to be found hanging around him, cadging rides. Dan did his share of hanging around, too; he enjoyed the rides when he got a turn but he wasn't interested in the bike itself, and he found the intervals of waiting so boring that his feelings about Terry and Jenk — his closest friends for years — had become decidedly mixed. Daisy went to the house of her friends Patsy and Monica and joined them in making a giant map of their imaginary country (called Hugoland after its dark, romantic king). But somehow this occupation seemed less engrossing than usual.

'What weapons do Hugo's army use?' she asked idly, drawing in fiddly islands off a rocky point.

'Move your elbow — it's on the Downs,' said Patsy. 'They'd use muskets, wouldn't they?'

'Ordnance,' said Monica wisely. 'That's cannons. Huge cannon-balls would crash into the fortifications.'

'Not bows and arrows?' said Daisy wistfully.

'Not at this time,' said Patsy. 'This is Hugo the *seventh*.'

'Are there women in the army?' Daisy went on.

'Oh yes — let's say there are,' said Monica with enthusiasm. 'They can have uniforms like the men, but with long, wide skirts; and ride side-saddle.'

'And Princess Felicia can be colonel-in-chief of the Reds, and lead a charge of cavalry,' said Daisy. 'Would you like to be in a war? Really, I mean?'

'Well, of course not,' said Patsy and Monica together. 'Blood, and ghastly rations.' Daisy was a little cheered by this confirmation of her views; but somehow she still managed to keep the secret of the discovery of the tree-people. She felt convinced that to talk about the tree-people would be very unlucky indeed.

There were no more manifestations from the Forest that day, although one odd thing did happen. The children arrived home at different times, Dan (streaked with grease) in time for late tea and Daisy (painty) for early supper. Mrs Sturgess told them both off for leaving the front door open when they went out, and they both denied it.

'I went out the back,' said Daisy; and Dan argued, 'I did go out the front, Mum — but I banged the door after me. I remember the bang.'

'Somebody left it open,' said Mrs Sturgess to each twin. 'And somebody has pulled half the clothes off the hall-stand and left them all over the place. Your anorak was on the floor, Dan. And dead leaves lying around.'

Both children felt uncomfortable; Daisy felt even more so when she got up to her own room. Her wardrobe door was open and there was a young, green lime-leaf on the floor beside it.

Even more worrying was Daisy's awakening next morning. Her father tapped on her door at half-past seven; Daisy grunted but didn't move. Ten minutes later her mother's urgent voice came up the stairs, 'Daisy! You'll be late,' and she reluctantly sat up in bed. Propped against the foot of the bed, by the wide-open window, was a tall bundle, bound round with linen strings. It contained four spears, simple shafts of ash with pointed ends; a bow of yew; and a sheaf of eight arrows with goosefeathers attached, and tiny tips of stone.

Daisy shot out of bed like an arrow herself, and the bundle was concealed at the back of her wardrobe before any parent could come thundering up the stairs. She appeared at breakfast pale and distraught, and spilt her tea into her sausages.

37

Margaret, who didn't like to start the day by sprinting, had already left for the school bus when Dan and Daisy, humping their school cases, shut the door on shouted goodbyes.

'Listen!' said Daisy, gripping Dan.

'Let go, you oaf,' said Dan. 'We're late as it is.'

'This is serious,' said Daisy. 'My bow and things have come. In my room when I woke up.'

'Heck!' said Dan. 'Where are mine?'

'You'd better look — I bet they're here,' said Daisy. 'I'll run on and hold the bus.'

This was a hopeful fiction — the bus never waited. But it was late that morning; there was no sign of it when Dan panted up to the stop in the village street.

'Found!' he muttered to Daisy, ignoring a chorus of whistles and jeers from the other boys there. 'In the laurel bush under my window, leaning against the wall. I hid them a bit deeper and left them there. Sit by me on the bus — we've got to talk.'

'I've promised to sit by Monica,' Daisy began.

'Well, unpromise,' said Dan. 'You can sit by her coming home.'

The twins' sitting together called for jokey comment from everyone else on the bus.

'Give over,' said Dan to the assembled company. 'We've got a secret to discuss. Our birthday's in July.'

'What's it got to do with birthdays?' said Daisy under her breath.

'It has,' said Dan. 'This is my idea. We've got to get old Briggsy to give us a holiday project we can do in the Forest.'

'He never does,' said Daisy. 'It's always something in Melbury. He loves Melbury. We'll have to trail in on the bus exactly as if it were term.'

'We've got to persuade him,' said Dan. 'We're going to spend the summer holiday in that Forest, like it or not, and the only thing that will make it work is a project. We may have to ask for project things for our birthday.'

38

'No — I know what we've got to have for our birthday,' said Daisy. 'Track suits. Think, Dan. It won't always be hot enough for you to wear shorts, and me summer dresses; and we can't wear our jeans when it gets cooler. When all the metal bits went, they'd just fall off.'

'You're right,' said Dan. 'It's the kind they call jogging suits we want: with elastic in the trousers and jumper-type tops. Jenk's got one. And the kind of trainers that haven't got metal eyelets and tags. You can get them with plastic.'

'Or with the eyelet-holes direct in the leather,' said Daisy. 'Good thinking. Let's hope Dad's feeling rich! We'll tackle Briggsy at break.'

Mr Briggs, the twins' form master, was surprised to be approached at break by the Sturgesses, united (for once) in clamouring for a woodland project for the summer.

'I've planned you a really superb project in the town,' he objected. 'Tracing the sites of some of the vanished buildings — the town gaol and the moot hall and the butter cross. You'll enjoy it.'

'It's such a long way in for us, sir,' said Dan in suffering tones. 'You know it takes twenty-five minutes on the bus, and we can't get in free when the school bus isn't running.'

'We've just got interested in the Forest,' said Daisy with a fine show of enthusiasm. 'We'd like to do something on trees. Or the history of the Forest — the king's chase and all that sort of thing.'

'It could be interesting, I suppose,' said Mr Briggs. 'And you people from St John are right out in the sticks. All right, I'll talk to Mrs Stock about it, and we'll think up an alternative project.'

It was a few days before this plot of the twins bore fruit. But on the Friday of that week Mr Briggs announced the holiday project to the form: the vanished buildings of historic Melbury. The class, as always, groaned cheerfully.

'And this year,' Mr Briggs went on, 'there is an alternative project for the savage tribes who live in St-John-in-the-Wood

39

or thereabouts; and anyone else, of course, who prefers the wilderness to civilization. You can work on this: "The trees of Hartwood, and what they tell us about the history of the Forest and its types of soil". Don't scribble, everyone: you're getting a duplicated sheet with a reading-list. And would the Sturgess family please note: I want two projects, not one.'

Dan and Daisy were able to laugh at this, along with everybody else. They deliberately sat at opposite sides of the room and their work differed totally in style and method.

'It's coming out all right,' said Daisy to Dan as they walked home from the bus.

'Well, I hope so,' said Dan. 'We'll just have to hope, though, that nobody else in the village does the Forest project. They wouldn't half get in the way.'

'Get shot, most likely,' said Daisy. 'They won't, though, Dan. Can you imagine Terry doing a project in the Forest when he might be going in to Melbury every day? They'll all be the same.'

'True,' said Dan, cheering up. 'They hardly go in the Forest, any of them, now we've stopped playing Indians. The fishing's better in the fields.'

'So,' said Daisy, 'we really only want the birthday stuff.'

The twins' real birthday was three days before Christmas, so they had an official birthday in July, celebrated always on the first Saturday after the end of term. They already knew that they were going to have the jogging suits they had asked for. By public discussion of the forthcoming project they had also got promises of a book on historic woodland, and *The Oxford Book of Trees*.

The awkwardness of the situation lay in that the first Saturday after the end of term would also be the day when they were to start what Daisy called military service: when they were to expect the king's and queen's call to arms.

40

—— 6 ——

The mastery of the spear and the bow presented a bigger problem to Dan and Daisy than the organization of clothes, books and a project. They started with the idea that they could practise, after school and at week-ends, in the Forest itself; but after they had lost between them three arrows and a spear — disappeared for ever into bracken-and-bramble tangles near the Forest's edge — they decided they would do better with an open field to start with.

'But nowhere too public,' said Daisy. 'We can't use the recreation ground or the common. Everybody there is would see us and want to join in.'

'The churchyard would do,' said Dan. 'We could shoot at the gravestones. Only I suppose people would object. And ghosts.'

'I know the place!' said Daisy. 'The paddock up behind Patsy and Monica's — where they used to keep their pony before feeding it cost too much. Mr Markham had his goats in it earlier, but there's nothing in it now.'

'Won't Pansy and Monkey-flower come and interfere?' asked Dan. It was one of his jokes that because Daisy had a flower pet-name, all her friends must have them too.

Daisy predicted that Patsy and Monica would want to try their hands at archery but would soon lose interest.

'All right, then,' said Dan. 'All we've got to do is to smuggle the bows and stuff up there without anybody's seeing. We ought to be able to manage that.'

They didn't. Outside Fosters, loaded with their gear, they unfortunately met Mr Sturgess — just getting out of his car to open the garage gates. It was Daisy's bow which caught his eye.

'Good Lord, Daisy, where did you get that?' he said. 'That's not one of those piddling little things you made yourself — that's a real bow, risers and handle and all. Self wood, is it? Even so it will have cost a bit to buy.'

41

'It's yew,' said Daisy. 'Samara Ash lent it to me. It's all right, Dad. She's got lots more. This one's too small for her.'

'I've got one too,' said Dan. 'A bit bigger.'

'Well, it would need to be,' said Dad. 'Your arms are longer than Daisy's; you need a bow with more weight. If you've only borrowed them, they may not actually be the right size for you. You should have been measured for them. Arm lengths.'

'We were,' said Daisy, remembering the clothes on the hall floor and making a rapid guess. 'Sleeve lengths.'

'Near enough, I suppose,' said her father. 'But where are you going to shoot? Remember, those are lethal weapons you've got there. An arrow's got as much penetration as a revolver shot.'

'We're going to Markhams',' said Daisy. 'To their paddock. We've got your old dartboard for a target; and there's plenty of room. We've got more sense than to shoot each other, Dad.'

'And will the Markhams be there?' Dad asked. He meant Patsy and Monica's parents, but the twins thought he meant the two girls and their 'yes' was more reassuring to him than it should have been.

'Is it a proper archery club?' he asked. 'If so I'll be tempted to come along myself some time. I've still got my beginner's handbook, if you want a borrow.'

'Could you find it now, Dad?' asked Dan hopefully.

'Shouldn't think so,' said Mr Sturgess. 'But your mother might.'

He was right; Mrs Sturgess found the book after only a few minutes' hunt along what looked like a completely haphazard bookshelf. 'I sorted them all out when I spring-cleaned,' she said, 'or I'd be as much in the dark as you are. All the sport's at this end now.'

'Anybody could tell *your* job,' said Dan. 'Is Librarianship catching?'

'Part-time,' said Daisy. 'She's only partly caught it.'

42

'You'll catch it in a minute,' said Mrs Sturgess, flicking a duster at them. 'Get along out.'

In Markhams' paddock, the twins flung themselves down on the short but doubtfully clean grass (the goats had left smelly patches) and opened their father's book.

'Hey, look!' exclaimed Dan. 'We ought to have all this extra kit! Bracers — what are they, sleeve-guards? And tabs — a cut-down glove. Why didn't Oak and Ash send those?'

'Perhaps tree-people don't need them,' said Daisy. 'They aren't quite flesh-and-bone, I think. Not quite like us.'

'I wondered about that,' said Dan. 'But look at this diagram! Daise, we've been doing it all wrong. No wonder we couldn't shoot far. You don't at all face the way you're shooting, you stand sideways.'

'At right-angles,' said Daisy, grabbing her share of the book. 'And turn your head to the target. Those old bows we had were so small we couldn't have got it right anyway. And look here — you don't hold the arrow at all, the notch in it holds it on the string.'

'Nock,' said Dan. 'That's the word here. Quick, Daisy! Get your bow strung. We must try it out.'

It was an evening of almost miraculous discovery. Once standing in the right way and drawing the bow and string apart at full arm's length, till their right hands lodged under their chins and their shoulder-blades seemed to meet, the twins really began to shoot. Their arrows started to travel a good length, and to go more or less in the direction they were intended to. None of the Markhams, after all, was home, as the entire family had gone to the Markham grandparents for the evening; and the twins aimed, shot, shouted and rejoiced in their growing achievement until darkness and dew began to fall. They ran home glowing, and only half heard their mother's crisp remarks about their lateness.

Until the end of term, Daisy and Dan's homework came a poor second to their military training. They talked their mother into finding scraps of leather left from a past

43

leatherworking craze, and making them simple bracers (held on with thongs — no buckled straps) and tabs; they talked their father into setting up a target on the lawn and criticizing their technique. It was an especially thrilling time for Daisy. She had never excelled at any sport before, although she was an adequate rider; but she discovered in herself an ability to shoot instinctively: not consciously thinking about the placing of her arrow on the target, not deliberating over her drawing or the loosing of the shaft. She just felt, and her arrows went home. Dan found this galling. Up till now he had always assumed he could beat Daisy at any sport (except riding, which he avoided for that reason). After a while he spent more time on the spear than he did on the bow: here his good eye (he could throw anything with fair accuracy) came into its own unhindered by the mechanical elements involved in archery, and his greater muscle-power meant that he outshone Daisy with ease.

'It's a pity we have to do both,' said Daisy. 'I'll never make a spearman, but I could shoot all day. I do think, though, Dan, we ought to practise hitting moving targets.'

'What, the Markhams' goats?' said Dan. But he put his mind to inventing a pulley system which got the dartboard to travel along the washing-line, while one or other twin shot it with arrow or spear.

'Provided the enemy looks like a dartboard, we should be reasonably O.K.,' he said cheerfully. Both children were silent for a moment, remembering with unease that for Daisy the enemy included Dan; and for Dan, Daisy.

All this time they heard and saw nothing of the tree-people; even on their trips into the Forest they saw nobody but the occasional human being.

'Do you suppose they've forgotten all about us?' said Dan on the last day of term. 'Or that the seeing-and-hearing effect has worn off?'

I shouldn't think so,' said Daisy. 'Don't forget they're busy: they're already at war.'

'I wonder why they want us anyway,' said Dan, repeating a question the children had argued over before. 'Even though you're a good bowman, we shan't be a lot of use to them. Unless it's still the fire business.'

'That's my guess,' Daisy agreed. 'They could use fire as a weapon if they wanted to. I think they want it in reserve; and to make sure each side has it.'

'It can't be that simple,' said Dan. 'They only wanted matches for their ceremonial fire, because they had to strike it quickly. They can make fire with sticks or stones for themselves if they need to.'

'You might need it quickly in war, too,' said Daisy. 'To surprise the enemy.'

'I suppose we'll find out,' said Dan. 'I wonder what the calling will be this time.'

'I'm not going to wait to be called,' said Daisy. 'I'm just going to go.'

The Sturgess parents may have been a little disappointed at the children's asking, as a birthday treat, to spend all day in the Forest. It left everybody else emphatically out. But they loyally agreed to the choice, and said nothing of the family picnic, and visit to a distant safari park, that had occurred to them as a suitable good time.

'Well, they're twins,' said Mrs Sturgess tolerantly. 'It's rather nice, really. They haven't played together since they were about eight — it's been all Terry and Co. with Dan, and Markhams with Daisy. Good that they find they can be friends again, now that they're older.'

'Hope it lasts,' said Mr Sturgess. 'It's a grand day for them, anyway.'

Daisy and Dan went straight after breakfast, each with bow, arrows, bundle of spears and food; each wearing elastic-topped plimsolls, T-shirt and stretch-waisted shorts or skirt. They went silent and somewhat breathless into the patterned shade, and parted from each other as soon as they were in the ride between the beeches.

45

'Good luck,' said Dan in a whisper. 'Don't shoot at me!'

'Same to you,' said Daisy. She turned aside towards the river and Dan went straight on.

Dan went on ploddingly. His breakfast hadn't gone down very well and he got hiccups. 'The condemned man got hearty indigestion,' he thought bitterly. He listened for Daisy's footsteps, but she was long out of earshot. Unheralded, an arrow flew past his face and stuck, shuddering, in the trunk of a tree, with a horribly noisy impact. Dan stopped, stiff as a plank, and Oak himself came noiselessly out of the trees.

'Stocks and stones!' he exclaimed. 'I understand you are something of a spearman; but a woodman, never. You make as much noise as a horse, and your bow's unstrung. Into the trees with you. You've got everything to learn. And the first lesson is — never let yourself be seen.'

'I thought of that,' said Dan. He felt proud of the fact that his shorts were khaki and his T-shirt green. 'But I thought you'd be looking for me.'

'So I was — and so might the queen be,' said Oak. 'Except that we have a truce for the day, while our new recruits learn sense.' He pulled Dan to a halt in a wide clearing.

'Now, for a start,' he said, 'take your spear and hit Rowan, who is coming between the thorn trees.'

'What, in cold blood?' said Dan, horrified. 'I can't do that.'

'I don't suppose you can — but should like to know,' said Oak. 'Watch this. Rowan! Come running.'

Rowan obligingly ran towards them, and Oak in one smooth movement raised, poised and hurled his own spear. It took Rowan in the shoulder: he staggered, laughed, and pulled the shaft out with both hands. There was no blood.

'But he isn't hurt,' said Dan.

'Of course not,' said the king. 'Would a blow like that harm a Tree? But it can put him out of the war. Once hit in battle, a fighting-man can use only one arm — that means the spear and not the bow. Twice hit, he can use neither arm and is serviceable only as a look-out. Three times hit, he is out of the fight.'

46

'But then it's a game,' said Dan, bewildered.

'A kind of game,' said the king. 'Or a kind of sport. Aren't your wars the same? Fought by professionals, you said; and mainly, I gather, fought by men. That sounds like games, to me.'

'But people die in them,' said Dan. 'It's real.'

'Our battles serve their turn,' Oak said. 'They test the balance. Come further into the Forest now. We'll try archery.'

It was a long and exhausting day. The king expressed himself profoundly dissatisfied with Dan's prowess with bow and spear, but was so mild about it that he seemed to mean the opposite. He made Dan aim, over and over again, at moving targets. Dan hit the long-suffering Rowan once with an arrow, but only when he was at a standstill; and twice, moving, with a spear.

'There,' said the king. 'If this weren't a day of truce, and if Rowan weren't on our side, he'd be out of the war by now. Considering how short a time you've had to train, you aren't altogether hopeless as a soldier. Sit down now and we'll drink.'

Bramble appeared with a pitcher and a wooden cup, and Hazel and Dogwood (a black-eyed, bouncing person) with bowls of earth and eating-bowls. Dan ate his lunch, and the tree-people mixed their gruel as before.

'Why do you mix it?' said Dan.

'Questions again!' said the king. 'You can have another three. Some trees like an acid soil, some a soil with a lot of humus, and so forth. Some like several, in proportion. We please ourselves.'

'Oh, good,' said Dan, thinking of his project. 'And how long can Daisy and I go on seeing and hearing all of you? Does it wear off?'

'It lasts for a year and a day,' said the king. 'Always a year and a day.'

'Why the odd day?' said Dan, forgetting he was wasting a question.

'To allow for sidereal time,' said the king. 'Which makes the extra day in a Leap Year, for us as for you. If you don't know about it, ask somebody at your school.'

'I wonder what lesson it would be,' said Dan. 'Not geography; science, perhaps.'

'It's general knowledge,' said the king.

'We don't do that,' said Dan. 'Dad said he got all his general knowledge doing crosswords. He's an addict. That's why we twins are called Aidan and Diana —because of the anagram.'

'You talk in riddles,' said the king.

'More or less,' agreed Dan. 'I wonder how Daisy's getting on. I hope she's all right.'

Daisy had had much further to go than Dan before she met a tree-person. Going towards the river, she went through a much more open part of the Forest; she got very hot and her gear grew appallingly heavy. It must be the worst part of being a soldier, she thought: humping all that stuff around all the time.

A movement in the trees to her right alarmed her: she stopped to string her bow, and got an arrow in readiness. Before she had drawn the bow, two towering tree-women appeared, one on each side of her.

'Disarm: we're the queen's people,' said one. 'I'm Hornbeam; on your far side is Lime. You are to come to Ash.'

The queen was on the same level ground, near the river and near her great ash-tree, where Daisy had met her before. As soon as she saw Ash's erect and motionless stance Daisy realized that the queen was still angry with her. She hesitated.

'Come on: it's too late to draw back,' said Lime.

'You committed yourself when you promised her fire,' added Hornbeam.

'Well?' said the queen as soon as Daisy was within earshot. 'Do females fight? Or do they turn and run?'

Daisy had nothing to say. But the queen's sarcasm sparked off anger in her: an active anger. She fitted her arrow to the string, swung round — raising her bow as she turned — and let the arrow go. It went fast and straight and whacked into the queen's own tree.

'And that,' Daisy thought to herself, 'has finally torn it! She'll never forgive me now.'

'A better answer than I had expected from you,' said the queen. Daisy turned, questioning, to find Ash pleased and laughing.

'Welcome to the warrior-women,' said the queen. 'If you shoot so well in anger, you'll shoot even better cool. And now you must learn woodcraft. We'll begin.'

—— 7 ——

It was one of those long, hot, memorable summers. It was also the strangest summer of the twins' lives. Every day they set off armed with notebooks and reference books and maps and Mr Sturgess's binoculars; every day they stashed this equipment in a convenient hollow willow and took out spears, bows, bowstrings, bracers, tabs and the cross-belts and quivers of leather which the king and queen had provided. (The tree-people had leather and horn, from the deer in the Forest; and their own flax, or that sometimes grown on a neighbour farm, gave them the linen for their strings. They waxed them with the wax from the wild bees' nests.)

Every day the children were involved into the silent intensity of the Forest war. They hid, stalked, ambushed, shot. They were burnt as brown as Indians and grimed by earth, mud, moss and the dust in the bark of trees; they were scratched by rough branches and thorns, and bits of leaf and twig got into their eyes and mouths. Dan was bruised by a glancing blow from a spent spear; Daisy knelt so long on a sharp stone in a thicket that she cut her knee. They became as tough as old boots.

Their use and knowledge of their weapons improved. Dan could hit almost anything with his spear; he learned to use a small wooden shield which made him more confident about this sort of fighting. It wouldn't stop a stone-piled arrow or spear in full flight, but it would deflect one which was nearly spent. He learned never to look up if he heard the whirr of a coming spear or arrow: a missile near the end of its trajectory is travelling downwards, and your eye can be one of your most vulnerable parts. King Harold was not alone. But Dan hoped not to join him.

The king also taught him to use a short, very sharp dagger.

'But it's wood,' said Dan, when first presented with it.

'What else?' said the king. 'It's dogwood, used from first times to make spikes and skewers. If it comes to a hand-to-hand struggle, this can stab.'

Dan realized it could; after which he cherished it and took it home, hidden inside his T-shirt, every night.

For Daisy, it was a time of glory. Against all expectation of her own (or the queen's) war absorbed her totally. On the few bad days of the summer she faced the problems of shooting in wind and rain; in the steady stretches of still, dry, baking weather she crouched for what seemed like hours in bushes and then tensed, poised, and sent the shaft which perhaps put one of the king's men out of the war for good. Three shots of Daisy's accounted for the mighty Beech. Hugoland had no more of her attention; this battle was real.

On the first fighting day (the Sunday) when Daisy arrived for battle, Ash looked at her severely.

'What's the matter?' asked Daisy, who was correctly dressed in a brown-and-black skirt and a dark green top.

'Your hair,' said Ash. 'You can choose. Cut it off, or tie it up somehow. If you don't, I will. It's got to go.'

'But why?' said Daisy.

'Hair blowing in a wind will catch the eye of the enemy,' said Ash. 'Look at us.' All her troop had their hair neatly up in buns or wound round their heads.

50

Daisy did hers in a thick plait and pinned it up behind; Ash lent her horn hairpins of great strength. It stayed that way all summer.

From then on, Daisy thought shooting all day, and dreamed shooting all night; and she ate her evening meal every day (fighting ended, and the children were dismissed, at about six o'clock) in a silent daze.

'I don't know what's gone with Daisy,' said her mother to her father. 'She's not with us half the time. I'd think she was up to something, but she's out in the woods all day on this project. And Dan's there.'

'Dan's a bit strange too — edgy and restless,' said his father. 'But there can't be much wrong: they eat and sleep like troopers. Let them alone. They're growing.'

Dan's edginess was a complicated mixture of exhaustion and frustration. Dan had been playing war-games since he was six; and since he was three or four he had been involved in unorganized fighting with other children — a natural, no-rules fighting based on all-in wrestling and accompanied by howls and yells and shouts of 'wham' and 'splat'. This war of the Trees was nothing like his idea of war. The silence oppressed him; the lack of immediate grappling with an enemy oppressed him too. His dreams were about fighting, like Daisy's, but his were nightmares, when an unseen enemy attacked him but stayed always just out of reach. He longed for a good, noisy, thunderous gun to shatter the tension of the woods and turn the battle into a pounding, socking, joyful mess.

All the time, the children learned what Oak and Ash called 'the true mystery'. They each had three questions a day until they built up a knowledge of what was really going on in the world of the Trees.

The worst problem for both children was to distinguish at a glance — before the ready hand loosed the arrow or projected the spear — queen's Tree from king's Tree in the tangle and shadow of the Forest. To make a mistake and score an 'own

51

goal' would have been something fearful to think of. Daisy and Dan had to learn and to repeat over and over again a roll-call of Ash's women and Oak's men; and to learn too to match heights and distinctive features to the names. There were some basic rules about the tree-people which the children mastered at length.

'First of all,' Ash explained to Daisy, 'all the water-loving trees are mine — Alder and Sallow and Willow — because I hold the dominion of water. And because I hold the dominion of air, all those trees hold with me whose seeds are scattered by the wind. Think of the keys of ash and maple —'

'Samaras,' said Daisy, who had learned the technical word. She was delighted to have an excuse to use the queen's secret name.

Ash looked at her warningly. 'And the tiny, floating seeds of elm and birch,' she went on. 'Do you see?'

'Wind-dispersal,' said Daisy. 'Yes, I see. And all the others are the king's?'

'All that fall straight to the ground, or are dropped by birds,' said the queen. 'Nuts and fruits and berries. They hold with the king. You should never be guessing who is on our side: you ought to know. Repeat the roll-call.'

And Daisy struggled through it as best she could, not always in the same order: 'Birch and Silver Birch; Elm, Hornbeam; Maple; Lime; Alder; Aspen; two Poplars, white and black; Sallow and Willow. . . . Though I don't see,' she added once to the queen, 'why you have Aspen as well as the Poplars, when she's a kind of Poplar too, and Sallow as well as Willow when they're some sort of cousin. It's all so confusing.'

'Nothing in the Rising and Falling is simple,' said the queen reprovingly. 'The very large tree-families may send more than one warrior to my band, and several do. Learn the names before you study the natures.'

'Oh,' said Daisy. 'I see. I'll start again. Birch and Silver Birch; Elm; Maple —'

52

'Hornbeam,' said an affronted voice from where that very tall Tree stood leaning on her spear.

'And what about Larch?' Daisy asked with a sudden recollection of the water-dancing. 'I saw her once at midsummer and she's never come again. Why isn't she in the roll-call?'

Hornbeam laughed, briefly and bitterly. Ash turned a cold stare on Daisy.

'You have no need to mention her,' she said. 'Weren't you told she wasn't one of us? If you see Larch in the Forest you can shoot her or not, as you choose — it doesn't matter to me. And that's all the information I'm giving you about Larch.'

Dan learned a roll-call too, and struggled to match names to faces. Some he knew before the Forest war began: Beech, Apple, Cherry, Hazel, Bramble. But others took longer. The names began to stick to the people when they met in ambushes and shared water during a break: Hawthorn, Blackthorn, Whitebeam, Service, Dogwood. There were a few he never did become sure about.

And he too asked questions. 'What I want to know,' he said to the king as they had an 'easy' after a successful attack, 'is why your Trees are men and Ash's Trees are women. Because I've been looking in my tree-book and trees don't work like that. Each kind of tree has both male and female flowers; some trees even have both sorts on the same tree. And some flowers seem to be both sexes at once.'

'You're beginning to learn,' said Oak with approval. 'That school of yours will be surprised to find what you know. Trees choose which kind of person should represent them. The trees which hold with the dominion of earth choose the things of the earth. They choose rootedness, or might; they choose standing; they choose the heel. The trees which follow water or air choose leafiness, or light; they choose dancing, they choose the hand. One kind of being is best expressed by maleness and the other by femaleness. It's a part of the balance.'

'What balance?' said Dan.

The king sighed. 'So you don't know much, after all,' he said. 'The natural world is composed of balance and maintains balance. Because it must. What else is our war about?'

'Balance between what?' Dan persisted.

'Day and night. Dark and light. Winter and summer. Earth, water, air and fire. He and she,' said the king. 'And that was three questions. Pick up your spear!'

The children still, however, gave themselves frights by failing to recognize until it was almost too late a he-warrior or a she-warrior. Once Dan was crouching with Dogwood in the cover of a hawthorn spinney; he raised his arm and held his spear poised as a strange Tree appeared briefly between two of the thorns. Long dark hair, loose in a rich mass, told him this was a she: he was about to let the spear fly when Dogwood gripped his arm.

'No,' he said softly. 'Let her go. It isn't one of us. You don't want to start another kind of war as well as the one we've already got.'

'Who is it then?' whispered Dan. 'It's one of the queen's people, surely?'

'No, no,' hissed Dogwood. 'When we have a break, find somebody to tell you about the winter people. But it had better not be Oak: it would be asking for a burst of his temper, and although he is a king we love, his anger is a thing to dodge. Ask Mistletoe; he knows them best.'

Accordingly, when the fighting ended that day Dan looked for Mistletoe. The first few Trees he asked said they hadn't seen Mistletoe, but Service remembered that Mistletoe had been set to guard a stack of spare spears, near the king's oak. Dan hurried there, and found the spears forming a miniature wigwam around the tree and no sign of Mistletoe.

'Deserted his post,' grumbled Dan to himself. 'Trust Mistletoe. No, don't trust him. . . .' He decided to go for a drink before setting out for home, and headed for a spring which gurgled out of the hillside a little way below the oak. Beside its basin Mistletoe lay dozing, one hand in the trickling water for coolness. Dan plumped down beside him and Mistletoe leapt awake.

'Who is it? Who is it?' he said anxiously, shading his eyes against the dancing light sifted through leaves.

'It's me, Aidan,' said Dan impatiently, cupping his hands for a drink. 'Can I ask some questions?'

'I suppose so,' said Mistletoe. 'Not all questions get an answer.'

'Well, I want to know about the winter people,' said Dan. 'I keep hearing hints, but nobody tells me who they are. I saw one today, and Dogwood said —'

'Which one? Describe it,' said Mistletoe.

'A dark woman, lots of hair; fairly thin but looks tough,' said Dan.

'The queen!' said Mistletoe.

'No, no; I said dark. Nothing like Ash,' said Dan.

'The winter queen,' Mistletoe whispered. 'Talk soft, then. Oak won't tell you about them, but somebody should. All right. For a start, have you and your sister noticed, while you've been serving with Oak and Ash, that there are familiar trees missing from their armies? Trees you thought ought to be there?'

'Oh, of course,' said Dan. 'But Oak explained about that. Only the Old Ones, the original native trees who came as soon as the Ice Age ended, serve him and Ash.'

'True,' said Mistletoe. 'The trees men brought to the country late on aren't in his Council. That rules out the fancy garden trees.'

'And lots of narrow-leaved trees,' put in Dan.

'Ah,' said Mistletoe with a quick, sidelong look at him. 'You spotted that.'

'Oh, wait a bit,' said Dan. 'I think I see what you mean. All the trees serving Oak and Ash are broad-leaved trees, aren't they? With proper leaves, not needles? And they all shed their leaves during winter. So what does that mean, Mistletoe?'

55

'It means they lose their rule in winter,' said Mistletoe. 'Naturally. A leafless tree is withholding its energies, storing itself for its new growth. Its tree-being isn't bothering itself about the rule of the Forest. So by common consent, in winter the winter people rule for them.'

'Pine and Yew — they're narrow-leaved,' said Dan. 'And I suppose the other evergreens are in it too? I've seen Box and Juniper in the Forest.'

'It's a good thing we can't be overheard,' said Mistletoe, laughing without humour. 'You've forgotten the king and queen. Holly, of course, and Ivy.'

'Ivy isn't a tree,' protested Dan. 'How can it be queen?'

'And it's even more fortunate certain ears didn't hear you say *that*,' said Mistletoe grimly. 'Size isn't all that matters. Frequency matters too. You would be hard put to it to go to any decent wood in this country and not find ivy; though you can find one without oak or ash. You wouldn't call Bramble a tree either, would you? But there he is in almost every woodland, and one of the king's own men.'

'So they rule in the winter,' Dan said slowly. 'Does that make them Oak's and Ash's enemies? Why should it?'

'Not precisely enemies. Nothing like friends,' said Mistletoe. 'Now do you understand? I'm going back to my spears.'

'You'd better,' said Dan, jumping up. 'Fighting's over — someone will be coming for them. I'm off to find Diana.'

Daisy was at the hollow willow, tired of waiting for him. 'You've been an age,' she said. 'I nearly went home.'

'Quick, then,' said Dan. 'I've got things to say.'

Mrs Sturgess had got tea for them, but she and Mr Sturgess wanted to watch a quiz on television, Margaret was out, and the twins ate on their own. Dan, between chews, repeated Mistletoe's information, and Daisy was horrified.

'How shall we ever know who's who?' she said through a mouthful of spaghetti. 'It's bad enough having to sort out king's Trees and queen's Trees. If we've got the winter ones as well, we'll never get them straight. What's the betting I hit

56

this Holly by accident and get sent to the tower — or ice-house, or something?'

'The cooler,' Dan suggested. 'We'll just have to hope. At least there aren't very many of them, and they don't seem to be about very much — I wonder why?'

'Keeping out of the way of the summer Trees' war, sensible creatures,' guessed Daisy.

'Well, maybe,' said Dan. 'So why was Ivy out today?'

'Looking for you,' said Daisy, and made a Dracula face.

—— 8 ——

The next day was one of the few chilly ones: sunless, and with a sharp wind ruffling the foliage. The children set out for war in track-suits, Daisy rather white after a conglomeration of nightmares.

'Serves you right,' said Dan, 'for trying to put the wind up me. The biter bit.'

'Don't,' said Daisy. 'It's true I'm twitchy. But I know what I'm going to do. I'm going to find the very largest of the queen's Trees and ask if I can fight alongside her today. Then I'll have someone to ask about any strange Tree that turns up.'

'Crafty,' said Dan with approval. 'I shall, too.'

When the queen gave directions for the placing of her troops that day, Daisy found herself sent to the same area in the High Forest as Maple. The two of them were to watch a Tree-track (indistinct to human eyes) which twisted among the beeches.

'Suppose we stick together,' said Daisy, eyeing Maple's large bulk and square shoulders.

Maple shot her a penetrating glance.

'It could be useful,' she said. 'I'm fighting one-armed — I was hit by a spear-throw yesterday. We could cover the path from different sides.'

57

'I was thinking of side-by-side,' said Daisy. 'We'd be company.'

'Not enough cover,' said Maple. 'We shall have to lie flat, as it is.'

They found a place where the hollows of old badger-sets, and a thick undergrowth of brambles and hollies, gave a bit of protection, and stretched themselves out on either side of the path. It wasn't what Daisy had wanted, but she decided it would have to do. The morning wore slowly away with no sign of an enemy, and Daisy wondered why the queen had sent them there. She grew numbed and stiff and finally her broken night caught up with her: she half slept.

A long, soft hiss brought her awake again with a shock, thinking of snakes. Then she realized that Maple had hissed to attract her attention, and without moving her head she lifted her eyes. Slowly and noiselessly, two king's men were drawing in towards her — Apple and Elder; and she was aware as she caught Maple's eye that Maple could see others closing in on the opposite side. The ambush was ambushed.

'We're outnumbered,' muttered Maple. 'We must make a stand for it. Now.'

She and Daisy sprang up, whirled round to stand back-to-back, and took aim. Daisy was now confronting Service, Rowan and Whitebeam. Her first shot went wild, but her second caught Service and her fourth, Rowan. She had then to dodge to avoid a shot from Whitebeam, and her next two shots were off the target. Her seventh got Service again — he was out of the fight.

'I've only got one arrow left,' she said to Maple.

'And I've only got one spear,' said Maple. 'Run for it — go the way you're facing.'

Daisy loosed her last arrow, which was a near thing but just missed Rowan; and as she shot she began to run. Rowan had ducked to avoid being hit and Whitebeam had stumbled in running towards Daisy; Rowan hurled a spear at her but it went high and passed just above her shoulder. In the momentary confusion Daisy — running as she had never run even in

58

the fiercest hockey match — rushed between Whitebeam and Service and was away. An arrow came after her — too close, and her heart beat wildly — but there was cover nearby. She dived into a group of taller hollies and from them into a jungle of young oaks and limes. The noise of pursuers faded and after a while Daisy doubled back and headed again towards the High Forest.

When she came again to the holly grove she stopped in its shelter to get her breath and to take stock. She still had her bow, but no arrows and no spear. She would have to make her way as secretly as possible back to the queen's hall for new weapons. Unless she could meet another queen's warrior who could spare her an arrow or two.

A soft crackle right beside her — who would want to be so close, when the Trees fought always at spear's or arrow's length, never hand-to-hand? Daisy swung towards the noise but her attacker was quicker than she: she found herself grappled from behind by thin, ropelike arms; a hand gripped her neck; and long, snaky tendrils of hair blew over her face. She tried to shout, but only a croak came out.

'Good,' said a low, chilling voice. 'A fine place to find you! This way — come on.'

Daisy was dragged a few steps and heard, as she struggled for breath, her captor jump hard on a patch of loose earth. In a shower of clods and tiny stones, the two of them crashed through the ground where they stood and fell heavily into darkness.

The side of the hole grazed Daisy's arm as she fell, but at least the two falling bodies landed soft. They came down on what felt like a compost heap: it was springy and had the cool smooth feel of leaves. Daisy lay looking up and saw bright, pale sky, netted with ivy stalks, over her head. The other person let her go and Daisy sat up, shaking debris off and brushing her face clean with her hands.

'Did you mean to do that — fall through the hole?' she asked.

'Of course; it's a doorway,' said the other person. 'Not that it's always convenient to arrive in the dungeon. — Fir!' she added, in a yell, and the name gave Daisy an extra twinge of alarm. If Fir was there, she was among the winter people.

'You know me, I presume,' said the winter Tree. 'Ivy, the queen. Your brother met me; he will have described me to you.'

'Sort of, but I can't see you properly,' said Daisy.

Even as she said this there was a crunching rumble and light showed through a gap in one of the walls: a large slab of rock which was entirely blocking a doorway was moving on a pivot of stone. As it swung open Daisy saw that a huge tree-woman — as big as Oak himself — was moving it; she also saw that Ivy was a relatively small person, as thin as a girl, with fierce, black eyes lighting a pallid face. Ivy was smiling at her and Daisy did not like the smile.

'We shall have a pleasant conversation,' said Ivy, 'the three of us. I'm sure you have a great deal to tell me.'

Daisy glanced at Fir, who stood massive and silent in the doorway and did not look at all conversational. 'What about?' she asked.

'This and that,' said Ivy. 'But foremost, what you were doing in the summer people's war.'

'Fighting for the queen,' said Daisy.

'Oh, I knew that,' said Ivy. 'But with what?'

'The bow,' said Daisy. 'I'm no use with a spear.'

Ivy made an impatient noise. 'I didn't mean that,' she said. 'Are you telling me the queen conscripted you simply because you could draw a bow? There was something else.'

Daisy stood thinking. Would it harm Ash and Oak if she mentioned fire?

'And I don't mean your firebrands, either,' said Ivy.

'How did you know about fire?' demanded Daisy.

Ivy made her impatient noise again. It sounded like 'chuh'.

'Naturally I knew,' she said. 'What happens in the Forest that is not seen by the wren, and told to me? — My bird,' she added complacently.

60

'Why, do the birds take sides?' asked Daisy.

'Most of them go with the summer people,' said Ivy. 'Ground-nesting birds like larks with King Oak. Water-birds like dippers and ducks are Ash's and so are the tree-nesters. The beasts the same: burrowers like badgers hold with Oak; water-beasts like otter, and overground sleepers like squirrel and deer, with Ash.'

'Rabbits for Oak and hares for Ash,' said Daisy. 'Ash didn't tell me.'

'All this is beside the point,' said Ivy. 'Except that the wren chooses me — its nest-tree — and the robin chooses Holly. Red breast to red berries. You should have been taught. Ash hasn't educated you.'

Daisy was tempted to say 'chuh' herself.

'Well, if you know about fire, you know about everything,' she said. 'There isn't anything else.'

'You mean to keep a still tongue. I see,' said Ivy. 'If that's your choice, you can stay here until you feel more like conversation.'

Fir swung the door fully open (Daisy could see a dark passage beyond, lit by a flaring torch) and swung it shut behind herself and Ivy. Daisy was left on her own.

The dungeon was a shape Daisy described to herself as square with round corners; the hole in its ceiling came right at one side and the heaped-up material beneath this was broken-off ivy branches. Daisy sat on it and wondered how she could attract the attention of a kingfisher or a duck to convey her whereabouts to the queen. The thought of a duck in her prison made her laugh. Not the most probable bird. But could there be a wood-pigeon or a woodpecker somewhere around? She looked up at the latticed patch of sky and was startled to see part of the light blocked out by a head. The face was in shadow but she caught the gleam of red-brown hair.

'Is it Larch?' she exclaimed.

'Yes,' said Larch. 'But speak low. There may be one of my people on guard in the passage.'

61

'You're one of the winter people!' said Daisy.

'Of course,' Larch whispered. 'What did you think I was? What does Ivy want you for?'

'She wants me to tell her something, but I don't understand what,' said Daisy. 'At this rate, I could stay here for ever.'

Larch didn't reply.

'Larch,' said Daisy, with the stirrings of an idea. 'You came to the water-dancing. Are you — would you — you wouldn't get me out of here, would you?'

'More than my bark's worth,' said Larch. 'Would you, if you served Ivy?'

'Tell somebody I'm here, then,' said Daisy. 'Tell Ash or Maple.'

'I don't go near them,' said Larch. 'I'm not welcome.'

'Tell my brother, then,' said Daisy. 'You could do that.'

'I could do that,' said Larch and was suddenly gone. Whether she would really go to look for Dan, Daisy doubted. But she hoped for the best, and ate her iron rations (half a bag of glacier mints); her lunch had been left hidden near Ash's hall. She wished she had a watch with her. Surely Maple had reported back to Ash's hall to fetch new weapons; surely the queen's Trees knew by now that Daisy was missing?

'She'll think I've deserted,' Daisy said to herself. 'I wonder if she shoots deserters. Or drowns them in that awful pond.'

Her thoughts were interrupted by some rustling from above — footsteps? And immediately after, a shout, a swish of sliding, a clatter of falling leaves and earth, and Dan crashed through the entrance-hole and landed on the ivy-branches.

'Oh heck!' was all he said. Daisy had a lot more to say.

'Dan!' she exclaimed in a storm of anger. 'You let yourself be caught — now how are we going to get out of here?'

'Not my fault,' said Dan. 'I was pushed. I didn't know there was a hole in the ground, did I?'

'So much for Larch and her being friendly,' said Daisy bitterly.

'You don't know that,' said Dan. 'It wasn't Larch who pushed me.'

'I pushed you,' said a voice from above. 'Stand aside!'

Dan rolled off the pile of ivy and scrambled up fast, and a tree-being dropped through the hole and landed elegantly on his feet. In the half-darkness of the dungeon Daisy, whose eyes were used to the half-dark now, saw that he was of medium Tree-height, slightly built and very brown of skin.

'Now isn't this nice,' he said sociably. 'A little get-together. Both of you and all of us. We'll get the leafy dew out and enjoy ourselves. But not in the dungeon — though it's a very good dungeon, drained and ventilated and with people always dropping in. — Fir!' he shouted, just as Ivy had done; and the slab door swung open, grating as before.

'Fir, dear,' said the Tree, 'is Ivy in?'

'Yes, lord,' said Fir. The children exchanged a glance and Dan's mouth framed the silent word 'Holly'.

'Come along, then,' said Holly. 'Follow me.'

He took the flaming torch from its niche of stone, and led them along the black passageway, into a cross-passage which veered sharply left, into another which veered right again, and into a straight one.

'It's a maze,' muttered Dan, and Holly heard him.

'More of a mole-run,' he said. 'Clever creatures, moles. Don't despair — we're arriving.'

The place they were arriving in was a large room, almost completely circular, rock-floored and earth-walled. Five passages opened off it. There was no natural light, but a flickering as of candles from small stone cups set into niches in the walls. In hollowed tree-trunks set around the walls, several tree-people slept. There was a round table in the centre of the room, and near it an ash-strewn fireplace. Around the table high-backed chairs were set, and Ivy was seated on one of them. She gave Holly a sideways smile.

'Both of them,' she said. 'Good.'

'I thought we'd have a little party,' said Holly, rubbing his hands. 'Leafy dew. Some fungus. Do our visitors like fungus?'

'We've only got the dried,' said Larch, who had come in from one of the entrances. 'Most kinds are out of season.'

'Don't eat or drink anything,' Dan whispered to Daisy, 'or we're in their power.'

'No whispering,' said Holly in a sharp, unfriendly voice. 'Most uncivil. We like our guests to share both thoughts and food. Fetch it, Larch.'

'Shall we wake the sleepers?' said Ivy.

'Stir them up,' said Holly. 'We rest a good deal in the summer,' he explained to Daisy and Dan. 'Some of us don't care for the heat, and we all need our time off. And of course we lie low when our foolish friends are so stupid as to engage in wars. Lunatic enterprises, wars.'

Fir had come in, and she and Ivy woke five sleepers. Everyone sat at the table, but there was no feeling of festivity. It was more like an exam than a party.

The twins both refused fungus (which looked like lumps of black shoe-leather) and leafy dew.

'Toadstools and stuff are poison to us,' said Dan. 'And we're not thirsty, thanks.'

'Then we'll wait until you are,' said Holly. 'Here's health to the winter, and downfall in the spring.' He and the winter Trees all drank.

'These are my people,' said Holly, who seemed to be doing all the talking, indicating those around the table. 'Ivy you know — the queen. Fir and Larch you know. Juniper — Privet — Box — Yew — Pine.'

'My people too,' said Ivy with a cold look in her eye.

'Both men and women,' said Daisy. 'The summer people are divided up.'

'Our numbers are smaller, so we are better friends,' said Ivy. Daisy thought she wouldn't fancy Ivy for a friend.

'And now for some conversation with our guests,' said Holly. 'So nice you are both here. Which reminds me, Larch — how come you brought the boy so opportunely?'

Larch's face stiffened, but she answered at once. 'I came upon him in the Low Woods,' she said. 'The girl was here, so I knew you'd want him too.'

'Extremely well done,' said Holly; but his look was stony. Both twins wondered uncomfortably whether Larch had meant well by them or had deliberately led Dan into a trap.

'And now — Aidan, isn't it? — I'll repeat a question I'm sure your sister has already answered. What are you doing for the summer king?'

'Not much,' said Dan. 'Hitting a few people with a spear.'

'More than that,' said Holly. Dan was as puzzled as Daisy had been.

'Don't know what you mean,' he said. 'That's all. Except for one box of matches.'

'Do you think I'll fall for bluff?' said Holly. 'I know perfectly well there's something more.'

'There isn't,' said Dan. 'Why does it matter? You said you aren't in the war.'

'Certainly we're not,' said Ivy. She was gripping her goblet with clenched fingers. 'And neither should you be. That's the point. Human beings have no part in our affairs.'

The Trees round the table said, 'Yes,' and banged their cups down in thumping applause.

'That's not what Oak says,' began Dan, but he was shouted down.

'Who fells the forests?' roared Pine.

'Grubbing people up by the roots!' added Box.

'Burning and breaking,' said Yew.

'And ploughing up good forest land — all out of greed!' said Juniper.

'Hunger,' said Daisy. 'We can't eat earth.'

'You could eat a lot less than you do,' said Privet rudely.

'You'd better know once and for all,' said Holly, 'that you're not welcome in the Forest. We know well you're serving Oak and Ash —'

'With an obscene power,' Ivy put in venomously.

65

'— and for their purposes they tolerate you,' Holly went on. 'But when the long winter comes and the sunlight shrinks —'

'Enough said, Holly,' Ivy interrupted.

'Fair and good,' said Holly, subsiding a little. 'Oak and Ash are giving you some protection. But there's no real safety in the Forest for the likes of you. Enemies you are and enemies you'll always be. Understand that.'

'Warned off,' Dan muttered to Daisy.

'And now,' said Ivy, suddenly cheerful and cosy in manner, 'tell us what you are really doing in the summer war.'

'We have,' said Daisy.

'Everything,' said Dan.

'Liars, like all the human race,' said Ivy. 'Take them back to their dungeon. Let's finish our party without a hostile presence.'

The twins were glad to go, and followed Fir meekly enough — but only because Yew walked close behind them, and a try at escaping into hopeful side-passages was ruled out. The children looked with calculating interest at the other passages, nevertheless, and both caught a rapid glimpse of a small Tree with white-blond hair in one of them. Surely — Mistletoe?

—— 9 ——

Back in the dungeon, Dan and Daisy drew breath. Dan was sweating and Daisy shaking.

'Dead scary, aren't they?' said Dan. 'Now we know what it's like to be a despised minority.'

'Outcasts,' said Daisy. 'They certainly don't want us for witnesses. The problem is now, Dan, what we do about the war. Holly and Ivy may go for us if we keep coming to the Forest; Oak and Ash surely will if we don't.'

'Who are you most afraid of?' said Dan. 'In the long run, I'm more afraid of Oak than of Holly. I sort of respect Oak but Holly seemed. . . .'

'Bogus?' suggested Daisy. 'All that charm. I'm not so sure, myself: Ivy makes my spine prickle. But I like Ash; I shall go on fighting. We'll just have to see what Holly and Ivy do. I didn't understand all that stuff they said.'

'Obscene power,' said Dan.

'The long winter,' said Daisy.

'Poppycock,' said Dan, reviving a little. 'All said to frighten us. Now, concentrate, Daisy. How do we get out of here?'

'I never tried,' said Daisy. 'It's too far up and the walls are steep. And it's not light enough to look for footholds.'

'Hm,' said Dan, shuffling around feeling the earth walls. 'Smooth as plaster — not a cranny.'

'A rope would help,' said a soft voice from above them. 'It's coming down. It's tied to a tree at the top; roll it up and take it with you. Leave at once — the party's in full swing and Fir is still away from her post. — And don't mention my name,' the voice added. 'You don't know who helped you to escape.'

'All right,' said Daisy in a stage whisper. But they both knew it was Larch.

Fortunately both children could climb a rope. Dan did it the school's way and Daisy by some peculiar method of her own which Dan called the knock-kneed spider act. She went up first, and fast; and when she emerged into the holly grove there was no sign of Larch. Her own bow was there, where she had dropped it; and a little further away, Dan's spears.

The rope, which had a much more woody consistency than most ropes they had met, and appeared to be woven out of tree-roots, was coiled up and slung over Dan's shoulder, and the twins crept quietly away. There was no sign of Larch.

Not until they had walked about half a mile from the holly grove did they stop, to hide the rope under the root-arches of a beech tree, and dare to speak.

67

'Wonder if our own Trees have missed us,' said Daisy, speaking low.

'We'd better split up,' said Dan. 'We're consorting with the enemy.'

'Shall we tell Ash and Oak what happened?' Daisy asked.

'Better not, I think,' said Dan. 'What do you say?'

'I feel better not, too,' said Daisy. 'I'm not sure why. I'll head towards the river here; goodbye.'

Daisy — whose probable capture by Rowan and Whitebeam had been reported by Maple to the queen — returned to a hero's welcome and was congratulated on her ingenuity in getting away.

'It took me a long time to escape,' she said. 'I had to hide.'

'You acted wisely,' said Ash with her wide smile. Daisy thought of Ivy's chilling stare and caught herself feeling glad to be home.

Dan returned only to a strip-tearing-off from Oak, for having deserted his post. In spite of the total unfairness of this Dan said nothing. He was aware of a sympathetic look from Mistletoe, and wondered how Mistletoe managed to move so fast. Was he really as short-sighted as he said?

The next few days seemed dull by comparison with what the twins called dungeon day. They tried for a while to keep near the Trees of their own sides, for fear of the resentment of the winter people at seeing them still in the woods; but the winter people did not appear and only Mistletoe's pale eyes gazed at the children speculatively. They wondered about him, too.

August went by, with Daisy in a trance and Dan in a fidget. The Sturgess parents apologized to the twins and Margaret for not arranging a family holiday — Mr Sturgess's firm was threatened with a take-over and Mr Sturgess, the chief accountant, worked himself into frowning fatigue all day and brought a stack of paper home each night. But nobody but the parents had noticed the lack of a holiday. Margaret was off into Melbury to meet Jamie every morning, and Jamie came back with her to tea or supper every afternoon; she filled the remaining time with an effort towards next year's A-levels. As for the twins, they had forgotten that sea and moorland and lakeland existed. Their life was bounded and shuttered with trees.

September might have gone by in the same way — which would have spelt doom to Dan and Daisy's project, as school started again before the middle of the month. But on the last day of August, Daisy was shot.

It was her own fault. When it happened, she was hidden in a little hazel thicket. All the leaves around had now the deep green of late summer and the Forest was in its usual late-summer drowse, birds and insects hardly stirring. She was waiting for Cherry, whom she believed to be somewhere around, to come into sight; but in the end the heavy silence deceived her into supposing that he had gone away. Stiff and cramped, she stretched a careless arm out: and at once a shaft from Cherry's bow (he had not been hit at all yet, in spite of Daisy's efforts) went into it. The hit was on the outside of her arm, near the shoulder, and away from the most important blood-vessels. But there was a great deal of blood from the wound, all the same; and Daisy fell down and lay speechless.

Cherry had never seen human blood: he was at a loss what to do. He rushed away headlong to find Dan. And somebody else slipped out of the bushes and ran off at the best speed he could make, to tell the queen: Mistletoe, the ubiquitous Mistletoe; who haunted both camps, who carried messages between king and queen or queen and king, who was always lurking near the scene of a conference and who seemed to be a licensed spy.

Dan was intercepted as he ran to look for Daisy. 'By the hazel thicket,' Cherry had said. 'You'll know what to do, won't you? I'm going to tell the king.' But Dan was not yet anywhere near the hazel thicket when two tall people jumped on him out of the leafage: Maple and White Poplar, each carrying a spear.

69

'You are to come to the queen,' said Poplar.

'I'm going to my sister,' said Dan, desperately trying to get out of the grip of the two tree-women. 'She's hurt.'

'She's all right: the queen's got her,' said Maple. 'You're the queen's prisoner.'

They towed him between them to the waterfall, and hauled him up. Dan had never been in the queen's hall before, and even in his panic about Daisy he felt some interest in the vast, cool cavern.

Daisy was stretched out on the floor, and the queen was calmly pulling out the arrow, which she had broken.

'You've no call to be alarmed, Aidan,' she said, quite kindly, to Dan. 'She's not much hurt. I've sent Mistletoe to get woundwort leaves. Hand me the bowl of water there.'

She washed the wound, and as soon as Mistletoe brought the woundwort leaves she wrapped them round Daisy's arm and fastened them with twines of traveller's joy. Daisy began to recover, and pulled a face at Dan.

'Have you surrendered?' she said.

'No, I'm a prisoner,' said Dan. 'Is it awful, Daise?'

'Not as bad as you'd think,' said Daisy. 'I've never been shot before. I bet nobody in our class has been shot. It's quite interesting. You ought to give me tea with lots of sugar in it. Am I pale? You are, Dan. You look horrible.'

'I was terrified,' said Dan. 'I thought you'd die.'

'And have a military funeral,' said Daisy. 'With arrows fired over my grave, into the setting sun, and a roll of drums.'

'Don't laugh — it's serious,' said Dan. 'What are they going to say at home?'

'You are excused fighting until the wound is whole,' said the queen to Daisy. 'It won't take long to heal. And you, Aidan, can't fight again for the king, having been taken prisoner by me: not until I give you leave.'

'I wouldn't anyway. Not until Daisy's better,' said Dan. 'But how do we get home? Can Daisy walk that far? And what do we tell our family?'

70

'Diana will be taken home,' said Ash. 'As to the story you tell, I can't advise you.'

Hornbeam and Lime, two magnificently tall tree-women, made a bandy-chair for Daisy with their crossed hands. They carried her effortlessly between them, to the beech ride close to Fosters. Dan scuffled after them, soggy with heat and dejected by the sudden and frightening end of the adventure.

The Sturgess parents were angry and upset at Daisy's accident.

'I knew somebody'd get hurt,' said Mrs Sturgess. 'Whose arrow was it? Not yours, Dan?'

'No — somebody called Cherry,' said Dan.

'Careless little devil she must be,' Mrs Sturgess stormed. 'Weren't there any responsible adults around?'

'Of course there were,' Daisy said hastily, wondering at the same time whether her mother would consider the glittering Ash, laughing over a well-aimed shot, in that light.

'No more shooting for you two unless I'm there,' said Mr Sturgess when he came home. 'And I'm taking you straight to the doctor's, Daisy. I never heard of wrapping up a wound in leaves.'

'That's fair enough, Harry,' said Mrs Sturgess. 'Woundwort's an old country remedy. All the herbals have it.'

'Maybe,' said Mr Sturgess. 'But they should have had a proper first-aid box. And what about tetanus? Are you fit to travel, Daisy? Or does the doctor come to you?'

'I'm coming,' said Daisy; and went.

'Oak and Ash's loss is Mr Briggs's gain,' said Daisy to Dan the next day. 'We've got to do that project. I can write, if I keep my elbow still. We know quite a lot, from what the tree-people have told us. I can't draw, though. Can you get some photocopies done in the Library, from Dad's map and the tree-books?'

'Mum will,' said Dan, cheering up. 'We'll show Mr Briggs about savage tribes in St-John-in-the-Wood! Where's my notes?'

But by afternoon, Daisy was tired of her stiff writing and went on a visit to the long-neglected Markhams, to show off her bandage and to try Monica's silver nail varnish. Dan, to his own surprise, went warily into the Forest.

He went as far as the clearing near which he had met Oak on what he called call-up Saturday.

'I want to speak to the king,' he said to the silent woodland. 'Would somebody please tell him so?'

In only a few minutes Oak appeared, and stood looking at Dan gravely.

'Well?' he said. 'I'm sorry Diana is hurt. Is the arm mending?'

'The doctor called it a scratch,' said Dan. 'It wasn't, though. I came to tell you our parents cut up rough, and we can't come back — even when Daisy's better and the queen releases me. It's too risky. It's a game for you, but we bleed. It's life and death to us.'

'I thought human beings wanted their wars like that,' said Oak. Dan looked for a quizzical gleam, but couldn't detect one.

'I thought so too, I suppose,' he said.

'There's a balance even between life and death. We are here to serve it,' said the king. He spoke sombrely. 'Doesn't your religion teach you that?'

'That's another thing,' said Dan. 'I don't go much for religion. Marg does, since she had a boy-friend who rang bells — the one before Jamie — and she got interested. But I don't think you're in ours.'

'Oh yes, indeed we are,' said the king. 'We shared our worship once. You still acknowledge the birth of light, at midwinter; and the rebirth of earth and its creatures in the spring. You call it resurrection.'

'I don't think you've got it quite right,' said Dan. 'And anyway, that's only part of religion. There's all the human part as well. People, and how they treat each other. And God becoming man.'

72

'Very likely,' said Oak. 'We don't share that, of course. But we are all in the Rising and the Falling. That's God.'

'Do you mean the sun?' said Dan doubtfully, thoughts about creation and growth going through his head.

'No: I mean that which is perpetually making and unmaking, and itself being made and unmade,' said the king. 'The very heart of balance. And if you don't believe that your religion knows about me, look carefully in your church. My likeness is there.'

'And is it all right that we're not coming back?' Dan asked.

'You'll come back,' said Oak. 'But I understand your parents' fears, and yours. You needn't fight any more.'

'It's good of you,' said Dan. It sounded old-fashioned, but they seemed the right words.

He went home via the church of St John, but he couldn't find anything about trees in it except his favourite window: a memorial window to the dead of two wars. It showed a glorious tree, red-and-gold leaved, against a brilliant blue sky; white birds roosted in or hovered above the branches. Underneath, in the glass, was a short list of names and the text, 'The leaves of the tree shall be for the healing of the nations.'

The organist came in, carrying a toppling pile of music, and caught Dan contemplating.

'Hallo,' he said. 'What's it this time? Are you doing a project on stained glass?'

'No — it's on the Forest,' said Dan. 'Somebody told me there was something in this church representing — well, a tree-person.'

'Oh, you mean the foliate head,' said the organist. 'Nobody knows what they mean — a pre-Christian symbol of some sort. It's at the top of the last column on the left. Ours is a very fine one.'

Dan went to the place pointed out, and stared up. Looking down at him was a stone head, overlapped and surrounded with oak leaves; branches bearing oak leaves and acorns grew from its mouth. He had never seen it before. It could easily have been a likeness of the king; or another Oak King before him. He went home comforted, and was thoroughly wild and disagreeable until bedtime.

'What's got into you?' said Daisy, as she went upstairs to early bed. 'Are you training for the Aggro Olympics?'

'Celebrating,' said Dan. 'Our war's over. Even if theirs isn't.'

'I can't quite believe it's over yet — even for us,' Daisy said.

Autumn

— 10 —

Going back to school after a summer as conscripts was an anticlimax. School, even in a new class and with new work, seemed flat and grey. The only cheerful spot was Mr Briggs's praise of their projects (he was still their form-master, owing to a reshuffle after some members of staff had left).

'It's an interesting theory that the High Forest is the most ancient area of the woodland,' he said to Dan. 'But you're not claiming it's primeval forest, are you?'

'Can't be,' said Dan. 'For one thing, the earl had pannage for two hundred swine in the Forest. The pigs must have got into the High Forest and messed it up. I meant I couldn't find any signs of coppicing or pollarding — that's only negative evidence, but it's something; and a lot of the things you find in ancient woodland — like small-leaved lime trees, and wild service trees — are there. And I talked to a tree-expert in the Forest; he told me what he thought.'

'Ah,' said Mr Briggs. 'One of the Men of the Trees?'

Dan stared, at a loss. Could Mr Briggs possibly know about Oak and his men?

'The Society of tree-lovers,' said Mr Briggs. 'Some local people belong. The Head does.'

Dan was relieved. 'I don't think this man belongs,' he said.

'And in yours, Daisy,' said Mr Briggs. 'I should think you're certainly right about the site of the mill and the ford. What put you on to it?'

'Nettles,' said Daisy. 'No, seriously!' (when the class laughed). 'Nettles and elders. And then when I looked I found humpy places where old walls had been.'

'I must borrow your map some time, and go and find the hornbeams,' said Mr Briggs. 'I've never noticed them. Mrs

77

Stock says she's never seen them, either. She's looking forward to having you two for Biology, this year.'

Dan groaned, but it was routine. He felt that after half living in the Forest for five weeks, he might be rather good at Biology.

All the old occupations started up again for Daisy and Dan, and Daisy's damaged arm soon lost its interest for the class. Hugoland recaptured its charm, with a forced engagement between Princess Felicia and the sinister Archduke Claudius, and a palace revolution. Dan got into the colts football team and mortgaged his Saturday mornings. The Forest stayed quiet, peaceful and cool beyond Fosters gates, unvisited by the twins; until the Saturday in late September when their mother sent them blackberrying.

The children went off after lunch, into a dry and dusty afternoon. They had no intention of going right into the Forest, only of skirting the edges, where the best blackberries were ripening in full sun. All the same, they got into metal-free clothes before they went, and rejected the plastic bucket they had thought of as a berry-container — because the handle was held on with metal links.

'Think of the agony,' said Dan, 'if the handle came off when we'd got the bucket full. . . .'

Lured by better and better berries, they went gradually into the first scattering of trees. They were picking a few metres apart when Dan heard Daisy make a cut-off choking sound. He looked round, to see that she was being dragged by one arm head first into a bramble thicket. He dropped his bag of fruit and shot to help her.

'What's got you?' he asked, gripping her round the waist. 'What is it?'

'A hand,' croaked Daisy. She had gone yellow-white and was shaking.

'Rubbish,' said Dan. He shifted his grip and hauled on her captive arm. It came out of the brambles, and sure enough another hand was holding Daisy's and pulling her forwards.

Dan seized the strange hand by its wrist and flung himself back with all his weight. Unscratched, unruffled, Mistletoe emerged from the bush.

Daisy, enraged, hit him with her free hand, and Dan twisted Mistletoe's arm to get Daisy's hand out of his grasp. Daisy's hitting hand was bruised by Mistletoe's hard elbow, and his arm didn't twist as it should have done; still, he let go of her and stood calmly smiling.

'What do you want?' said Dan, blazing.

'Just a talk. Just a chat,' said Mistletoe. 'But not here. I'll show you where the blackberries are better.'

He led them right out of the trees and into the open of the lane which looped round towards Fosters.

'We've done this bit,' objected Dan, and Daisy added, 'The fruit's all gone from here.'

'I know,' said Mistletoe, in a whisper, 'but I want to talk to you away from trees. Somewhere on your ground — human ground — with plenty of metal.'

'But you don't like metal,' said Dan, also low.

'*They* don't like metal,' said Mistletoe. 'I can just tolerate it. I'm not quite one of them — remember?'

'I know, Dan,' said Daisy. 'The garage! The car's in.'

Inside the garage, Mistletoe looked with nervous terror at the car. The twins were not sorry to see him frightened: it was his turn.

'We'll get inside it,' said Daisy.

'Right inside?' said Mistletoe, hanging back.

'I thought it wasn't you who dreaded metal,' said Dan, giving him a half-friendly push.

The three sat in a row on the back seat, Mistletoe squeezed between the twins and smelling of green in the stuffiness. The incongruity of this conjunction of human world and Tree world was what Dan remembered years later as the oddest part of the whole Tree episode.

Once in the car, Mistletoe took courage. 'An elementary law you will find useful,' he said. 'The presence of metal

79

deadens the senses of the tree-beings. If you are completely surrounded by metal, you are neither visible nor audible to Oak and Ash and their cronies; unless they actually touch you, as I'm doing now.'

'Does it mean we can't see or hear them either?' asked Daisy.

'They wouldn't dare enter metal,' Mistletoe said. 'It doesn't apply. Even I wouldn't enter this hut-on-wheels if I weren't between the two of you.'

'Poor Dad's new car!' said Dan. 'What is this, then — a secrets session?'

'I have — a sort of offer,' said Mistletoe guardedly. 'I thought many times in the summer that both of you, Aidan and Diana, enjoyed fighting; but that you didn't enjoy fighting on different sides. Am I right?'

'I liked the fighting,' said Daisy. 'Loved it. Stalking, and shooting, and nobody's getting hurt. It would have been more fun if Dan and I had been together. I expect.'

'It wasn't my idea of war,' said Dan. 'Together or not.'

'And I think, too,' said Mistletoe, apparently ignoring their answers, 'that you have a reason to bear a grudge against both Oak and Ash. You were coerced into serving them; made to fight much to your own peril; and finally one wounded and one taken prisoner. You've got a score to pay.'

'It wasn't like that,' began Daisy, wondering quite why it wasn't. She only knew Mistletoe had got it subtly wrong.

'So why not,' Mistletoe went smoothly on, 'join with those who oppose both Oak and Ash? You could fight side by side. And you'd be rewarded. Oak and Ash offered you nothing and gave you nothing. Their enemies would give you power among themselves, in repayment for your help.'

'Enemies?' said Dan. 'You mean the winter people?'

'So you know what's in the wind,' said Mistletoe.

'We know who we're talking about,' said Daisy, 'but not what. Why should the winter people be fighting Oak and Ash?'

80

'They have increased,' said Mistletoe. 'Not naturally, of course; but everywhere you men cut down the old jumbled forests, oak and birch and beech and ash and hazel, and replant only with the winter people. They grow all the time — in numbers, but not in power. The balance is affected; the balance must alter. Now's the time for them to challenge the summer people for mastery.'

'And you think we'll help?' said Dan. 'For a reward?'

'They're prepared to offer you some proportion of their power,' said Mistletoe. 'They'll talk to you about it.'

'I thought they wanted us to keep out,' said Daisy. 'Anyway, I won't fight for them. I made a promise to the Ash Queen; an oath, perhaps — I'm not sure where oaths begin. I told her I'd help her. I won't change sides.'

'It wasn't the same for me,' said Dan, awkwardly. 'I never chose to fight.'

'Yes, you did,' said Daisy. 'You sent a message saying Aidan Sturgess would serve Oak as spearman and bowman. Mistletoe remembers.'

'I'd rather forget,' said Mistletoe stiffly. 'I see. You stand by the summer people, then — Oak and Ash.'

'Yes, we do,' said Daisy, and Dan nodded — a little reluctantly. He was not anxious for any more spear-and-bow work among trees.

'You'll regret it. If you live to,' Mistletoe said. 'And now, we'll be going.'

'Back to our blackberries, you mean?' said Dan, scrambling out of the car.

'To Oak and Ash. I was sent to fetch you,' said Mistletoe.

'I didn't like the way you did it,' said Daisy, following him out. 'What's to stop me from telling Ash what you said to us?'

'Do as you like,' said Mistletoe.

'Why bother?' said Dan, stretching. 'They know he's a spy.'

In a silence of dudgeon, Mistletoe and the twins went back to the confines of the Forest. They were hardly inside its edge before Mistletoe flung up his arms with a shout, 'Queen! We are here!'

Daisy, guessing what would happen, gripped Dan. The uprush and surging along of air swept up both the children, lifting them off the ground as it had done Daisy on Midsummer Night. This time Daisy was able to enjoy the feeling completely; and Dan yelled with the thrill of it. It was flying without the effort of self-propulsion, the drag of heavy wings against a jutting breastbone, and without the encumbrance of machinery or any gear — it was absolute freedom. The air roared and sang around them and they laughed, exhilarated by their speed.

When the roaring began to decrease and a sensation of falling set in, Daisy called to Dan, shouting into the whirlwind, 'Watch out! We may land on water.'

But they didn't: they landed on the gathering-floor of the Trees, the fire-place, near to the central stone with its covering of charred flakes and ashes; and Ash herself came forward to welcome them.

'You're summoned to celebrate with us,' she said. 'Today we make peace, and there are songs and dances and a feast.'

'Peace!' said Daisy, considerably startled. 'Is the war over?'

'— Who won?' interrupted Dan.

'Nobody won,' said the queen, smiling. 'We were evenly matched. Almost simultaneously we lost our last spearman on each side.'

'And so peace is declared,' said the Oak King, speaking from where he stood on the far side of the fire-stone.

To his surprise, Dan found himself profoundly happy and satisfied to see Oak again. 'It's just as well,' he said to Oak. 'I couldn't fight for you any longer, in the war. What would you have done if you'd won?'

'Given more power to the queen,' said Oak decisively.

'*More* power!' exclaimed Dan, shocked. 'But if you'd won, you could have taken her power away.'

'You speak as an animal,' said the king kindly. 'You animals fight for territory and leadership. We trees who hold the balance fight to preserve the balance. If the war had proved the queen to be weaker than I, I should have given her some of my people, or a greater share of the dominions. She would have done the same for me, if she had won. Balance would have been restored.'

Tree-people came crowding round the fire-stone bringing branches and kindling and building up the fire. While the Trees were all busy and active, Daisy drew Ash aside and whispered to her.

'Queen!' she said hurriedly. 'The winter people are plotting against you. You ought to know.'

'But that's to be expected — it's the time of year,' said Ash. 'They always conspire in autumn. It means no harm. It doesn't threaten the balance.'

'But it does,' Daisy insisted.

'No, no,' said Ash soothingly. 'You'll see later. And understand.'

When the fire was laid, Oak and Ash brought their boxes of matches out from inside their tunics and ceremoniously lit it. Flames danced up in the dry warmth, and the king and queen moved together and exchanged a formal kiss of peace.

But it was something more than that. As they moved apart they smiled at each other with a smile of such delight that Dan dug Daisy in the ribs and whispered, 'Funny!'

'Yes,' Daisy whispered back. 'You'd think, wouldn't you, they'd really been friends all the time.'

—— 11 ——

It seemed to be expected by Oak and Ash that the children would stay with them and share the rest of the celebration.

'I'm afraid we can't,' said Dan politely to the king. 'Though it's kind of you to ask us. Our mother sent us to get her some blackberries, and she and our father will be expecting us home.'

'They'll be worried if we don't go,' added Daisy.

'It's a pity,' said the king. 'As well as missing our peace festivities, you'll miss the autumn festival. It's the festival of the earth. We have a meal of the fruits of the season — apples and nuts and berries, things you would enjoy — though we ourselves only eat them once a year. We share them with the birds and beasts, who come to us here at dusk. And we beat the bounds of the Forest, going around it all night long with torches and songs and marking our special boundary places with the chosen stones. Underground, as well, where the caves are.'

'We certainly can't stay all night,' said Daisy. 'Not this time. We'll come another time, if you are so kind as to invite us and we can get away without being seen.'

'Is it a law,' said the queen, evidently inquisitive, 'that children do as their parents want?'

'Well, it isn't a law,' said Dan thoughtfully, 'it's a sort of understanding. We're too young to earn our own living, so they give us home and food and look after us and we do what they tell us — most of the time.'

'It's a bond,' said Daisy. 'But don't you know about it? You have seedlings from your different kinds of fruits, and new trees grow.'

'The parent-child bond is unknown to us,' said Ash. 'The wind takes my seeds; my offspring may grow half the Forest away. I shouldn't recognize them. They fend for themselves.'

'But your acorns fall straight down,' said Dan to Oak. 'You must know which they are.'

'They're often moved away,' said the king. 'By birds or animals, or passing men. If they tried to grow up directly in my shade, they wouldn't prosper, for lack of light. It has no special meaning to me if a shoot grows from an acorn of mine. All oaks are oaks, and related to me.'

'But the tie you've described is a kind of law,' said the

queen to Dan, 'and we respect it. If you were meant to take home blackberries, we'll give you some of ours as your share of the feast.'

'And you'll come to our mystery in November, after leaf-fall,' said the king. 'Remember!'

Daisy and Dan went home — attended part way by a singing escort of Poplar and Rowan, with Silver Birch dancing a twirling dance of her own and turning cartwheels in front of them. They took wooden pitchers, full of blackberries of great size and lusciousness — complicating their lives by the fact that the pitchers had to be smuggled into and out of the house and hidden the far side of the garden fence.

'It must be a marvellous year for blackberries!' said Mrs Sturgess, delighted with their haul. 'I haven't seen such beauties anywhere. I was thinking it has been too hot a summer for the fruit to be good. Take a few of these, Daisy, and run round to the church with them. Margie's helping to decorate for Harvest Festival tomorrow.'

Both the children went, and admired the decorations. Dan borrowed the decorators' ladder and climbed up and put a little wreath of bryony round the foliate head that he thought of as Oak.

'Oh, are you trimming up the Green Man?' said Margaret, looking up. 'Pagan thing! I don't think it deserves it.'

'It isn't pagan,' said Dan, incensed. 'It's to do with the creation part of religion. The rising of the sun, and the turning of the year,' he added, vaguely.

'To me it's the demon king appearing in the woods,' said Margaret.

'You ought to have grown out of pantomimes by now,' said Daisy in a down-to-earth manner, looking warningly at Dan. 'I'm going. I've got homework.'

'I wonder what this leaf-fall do of the Trees is like,' said Dan as they idled their way home.

'Not till November,' said Daisy. 'But some of the leaves are down already. There are a lot off the limes by the church, and the horse chestnuts at school.'

'Not off the oaks, though,' said Dan.

That autumn Daisy and Dan both watched the changes in the trees with vivid interest. By October, acorns were falling and the lime-fruits dried up on their long wings; the ash keys made heavy, brown clusters. Not many leaves had fallen, though they had changed from green to yellow and gold. By early November, the limes were almost bare and the ash-leaves dropping fast, though the oaks were still in rich brown leaf. But November was windy, and by its last Saturday there were only a few leaves left, on the lowest branches of the oaks and beeches; most of the other trees were bare now, and there was thick leaf-litter on every patch of Fosters' lawn.

That last Saturday was stormy, with sharp showers of rain driven by whips of wind. Both Dan and Daisy had the fidgets.

'Will they call us? If it's today?' Dan asked Daisy as they shared the breakfast washing-up.

'It must be today or tomorrow, if it's during the daytime,' said Daisy. 'They know about school.'

'I want it to be today,' said Dan. 'Let's get dressed for it. No-metal clothes take some thinking about. And let's get sandwiches made.'

No-metal clothes weren't too difficult. Track suits, duffel coats and wellingtons. 'Thank goodness there's no iron in wellies,' said Dan, pushing in his almost-too-large feet and stamping down.

'Oh, are you going out?' said Mr Sturgess hopefully, appearing in the hall doorway with a load of paperwork. 'You might rake the leaves off the lawn, if it's your day for doing good deeds. Double pocket-money if you get them all.'

'Race you to the leaf-rake!' shouted Dan to Daisy. As he started first, he got it without difficulty, and Daisy had to settle for the weeding-rake.

'Of course, if I were Oak, I'd give you the leaf-rake — because I won the race,' said Dan.

'Let's fight for it,' said Daisy. 'Rake against rake.'

86

The fight was inconclusive, because the head flew off the weeding-rake and some of the prongs of the leaf-rake got extra bent. Daisy and Dan got down to the job instead, and soon found that one raking and one wheelbarrowing was the best division of labour. As Daisy was approaching the compost heap with a loaded barrow, she looked up and saw Blackthorn and Hawthorn, two of the king's men, standing silent on the far side of the fence, looking at her.

'Is it a summons?' she said, stopping dead.

'Yes, we're the summoners,' said Blackthorn. 'You've to come.'

'We're more or less ready,' said Daisy. 'We've got sandwiches.'

Dan looked up, hearing her speak, and saw the two Trees.

'O.K.,' he said to Daisy. 'That means Oak. I'll put away the tools; you get the food.'

To the children's disappointment, this was a walking journey, not a whirlwind one. Much of the time they plodded along in silence, as the going was unpleasant. Rain came on, and they had to watch their wellingtons in the slithery mud.

At the top of a hilly bit Hawthorn called for a breather: the children needed it, although the Trees didn't.

'You'd better not arrive too exhausted,' said Hawthorn. 'You are the witnesses.'

'Yes — but why? Why do Oak and Ash want witnesses?' asked Dan, between puffs for breath.

'There should be witnesses in every generation, so that human people can take part in our affairs and understand the things of the trees,' said Blackthorn. 'In the old days, children were exchanged. A human baby would be brought up in the woods, and a Tree-child in a human family. The custom died out: the human parents came to resent it.'

'Because of the parent-child bond,' said Daisy. 'Didn't the exchanged children ever want to stay where they were, when they grew up?'

'Sometimes,' Blackthorn said. 'A human child might love a

87

tree-being, and want to be married. That didn't work the other way, of course; Trees don't have marriage, or that kind of love.'

'Or a human child might love the woods,' said Hawthorn. 'And return to them; as the great Robin did.'

'Robin Hood!' exclaimed Daisy.

'Robin Wood,' said Hawthorn.

'But why us?' Dan asked, hammering away at his point.

'Why not you?' said Hawthorn. 'You're here; you spend a lot of time in the Forest. And you are children: you can't be blamed for what the human race has done.'

'What did we do?' asked Daisy, a bit huffy.

Blackthorn answered, speaking gruffly, his thin face scowling. 'Your hurry and greed brought the elm disease, the great elm death.'

'And your greed plants everywhere the fast-growing trees — not the trees of our native soil,' said Hawthorn. He sounded almost dangerous. 'Not our fine old spreading forest trees. But the narrow-leaves, the softwoods, the quick ones. That is, of course, where you're not grubbing woodland out altogether and putting crops or houses in. Either way, the balance goes.'

'Daisy and I never did anything like that,' said Dan. 'We've planted acorns and conkers. We cut down a fir-tree once, when we wanted a Christmas tree and Dad forgot.'

'Cutting down a tree — any tree — doesn't do you credit,' said Hawthorn severely. 'On the march again, now; they'll be waiting.'

Rain began again, and in the face of a bitter squall the children battled the last mile to the gathering-floor. On the edge of it, they stopped, startled. In the wide clearing stood their old friends and companions, dressed in their formal robes — the people of Oak and Ash. But at the centre of the circle of Trees, nearest to the fire-stone, stood other people they knew: the inhabitants of Holly's and Ivy's hall.

'The winter people!' whispered Daisy.

88

'It must be nearly their time,' Dan muttered back. The two children looked with curiosity at the small group of winter people around the stone, now that they saw them in daylight. 'They're only a gang,' said Dan. 'Hugely outnumbered.'

'Even though they let Trees which aren't Old Ones fight,' Daisy agreed. 'Fir and Larch aren't — did you realize?'

They studied most of all Holly's wiry strength and sparkling black eyes, and the pale-eyed, black-haired Ivy, beautiful and strange.

Although the winter people were so much in the forefront, Oak and Ash still seemed to be in charge of the proceedings. They welcomed the children, and showed them how to do a swaying, stamping dance which wreathed its way around the stone. The winter people made an inner circle which at times danced its way among the outer Trees in a winding chain. Daisy noticed, with foreboding, that Mistletoe danced with the winter Trees.

At the end of the dance, Oak and Ash as usual lit the branches heaped on the fire-stone. There was more dancing while the fire blazed up. The wood and brushwood must have been protected from the rain, as they burnt well. The last few drops of the storm fizzled into the flames, then the rain conveniently ended. Almost simultaneously, the dancing stopped and a dead silence fell. The tree-people took up places around the roaring fire: winter people again in the centre, Oak and Ash among them, standing side by side; then a space, and then the summer people on the outside of the ring, where the Forest began again. There was a feeling of strong suspense, of held breath.

Oak and Holly stepped up close to each other.

'Your time has come,' said Oak. 'In the Rising and Falling, strike your stroke, Winter King. And rule the Forest by my laws, and in my place. The dominion of earth is between us.'

He pulled from his neck the flat, pierced pebble, on its string, and tossed it on the ground between himself and Holly. He knelt down, watching Holly intently.

89

Holly made a sign to Mistletoe, who came up to him and put into his hand an axe. It had a wooden handle, but fitted into this was a head of stone, chipped to a sharp cutting edge.

Daisy, sweating with apprehension, moved close to Dan and gripped his arm. 'Dan!' she whispered urgently.

'Shut up,' Dan whispered in return. 'We can't stop it.'

'My time has come,' said Holly. He spoke without exultation, but with a kind of solemn pride. He swung the axe, with no visible effort, and with a sideways swiping blow struck Oak's head from his body. The body fell where Oak knelt, the head several metres away. Holly picked up the fallen pendant from the ground and put it on. 'I hold the dominion of earth,' he said into the silence. 'I am the Winter King.'

The winter people cheered and the summer people gave a single, loud, protracted groan. Dan and Daisy clung together.

'I don't believe it's what we think, Daise,' murmured Dan. 'He isn't human. Look, there's no blood.'

'But trees die from axes,' said Daisy, hopelessly. 'He's dead. The king's dead.'

As if to reinforce his words, Holly and another winter person lifted Oak's fallen trunk and flung it into the blazing fire. A third did the same with his head. A sigh went up from all the summer people, but nobody moved to interfere.

Ash now stood forward and walked up to Ivy. 'It is your time also, Winter Queen,' she said. 'In the Rising and Falling, take the dominions of air and water; rule well for me.' She gave her single butterfly-wing ear-ring and her pearl ring to Ivy, who without speaking put them on.

'— For,' finished Ash, 'it can never be that I should live and rule without my companion king!' And with a spring she hurled herself into the blaze of the fire. Her body lay beside Oak's. Strangely, they looked now like two great logs, two fallen tree-trunks, not the beings Oak and Ash whom the children knew. All the same, Daisy was crying and Dan, tense and miserable, hugged her for his own comfort as much as hers.

Now, what seemed an atrocity, the tree-people began to sing. The winter people started it, but the summer ones joined in. For the winter people, it turned into a dance; a twirling, leaping, jubilant dance round the funeral pyre of Oak and Ash. To the children's horror the song was — almost — one they knew.

> The holly and the ivy
> When they are both full grown,
> Of all the trees that are in the wood,
> The holly bears the crown:
>> The rising of the sun
>> And the running of the deer,
>> The playing in the merry morning,
>> Sweet singing in the brier.

'They've altered the words,' said Daisy, wiping her eyes and nose messily on the back of a woollen glove.

'No — we have,' said Dan. 'Marg says it's pre-Christian.'

'It doesn't mean anything,' said Daisy.

'Animals play in the morning, birds sing in the brier,' said Dan. 'Listen — the verses are different, too.'

'I want to go home,' said Daisy desolately.

At the end of the carol, the summer people slipped away, by ones and twos, into the surrounding Forest.

'You are the witnesses,' said Holly courteously to the children. 'Ivy and I are going now, with the symbols of our rule, to our own hall. You must be our guests.'

'No!' said Daisy vehemently.

'My sister means, we have to go,' said Dan more diplomatically. 'We have to finish a job at home.'

'As you wish,' said Holly. 'You've seen the heart of the matter. Hard words were spoken when we met before: let them be forgotten. You'll be as welcome to the Winter King as you were to Oak, when he was in power.'

'And to the Winter Queen,' said Ivy, equally polite. 'The

winter woods are less inviting, but we have our feasts and festivals just as the summer does.'

'I won't go near them,' said Daisy savagely as the children stumbled home alone through renewed rain. 'Never! They killed the Oak King.'

'I wish I understood,' said Dan. 'I don't though. One thing, Daise: I'll never enjoy Guy Fawkes again.'

He wished he hadn't said it, as Daisy replied by a fresh outbreak of sniffs.

Winter

—— 12 ——

The excited trepidation which had been Daisy's and Dan's main attitude to the Forest all summer was now something different. Daisy felt a real horror of the winter people and wouldn't set foot inside even its outer fringe of trees. Dan was nervous of the Forest, although he didn't share Daisy's view of Holly as an assassin. Oak had seemed to him to die willingly. If he were really dead.

During the next few weeks the twins continued to keep out of the woods. Mr Sturgess, emerging from under his load of paperwork as his firm's affairs settled down, several times proposed walks at week-ends. There was always a reason why the twins found it totally unsuitable to go into the Forest: excessive mud, loss of wellingtons, desire to see the Markhams' goats (in the opposite direction); anything went. Once when Mr Sturgess insisted that only the Forest would do, Margaret and Jamie were the only people to go with him, the twins having had a sudden and severe attack of homework.

One quite unexpected encounter they did have, and it unnerved them even further. A lost ball — shot over the garden fence in a game of three-handed rounders — had to be retrieved.

'I'm not going,' said Margaret, who had pitched. 'I don't want my tights torn on the brambles. You hit it, Dan, and you're in jeans. You can go.'

'Come and help, Daise,' wheedled Dan. 'You're in jeans too.'

The other side of the fence the outposts of the Forest began, with small ash-trees, birches, and liberal growths of ivy. The children scuffled and peered, unwilling to go very far from the house. Margaret gave them up and went indoors.

'We'll never find it,' said Dan, beginning to get bothered.

95

'It's here,' said a quiet voice, and Dan and Daisy shot upright, to find they were looking at Larch. She came out from behind a poplar and the ball was in her hand.

'Oh — Larch!' said Daisy, relieved. She held out a hand for the ball.

'Come to the fence — I've something to say,' whispered Larch. 'The fence is full of your human nails; we won't be heard.'

'But can you stand it?' asked Dan.

'Only for a moment,' said Larch. 'I can't hear well near it, either: whisper close to my ear.' She put a hand on the fence, and whispered herself. She shivered and shook even as she spoke, with horror at the iron so close to her.

'I mean you no harm,' she said. 'Don't blame me that Aidan was caught in Holly's trap: I thought Holly safe in his hall, and was off my guard. I've something to say to you. Don't trust Ivy and Holly when they seem kind. What they told you in their hall was the truth: they hate the human race and they hate the summer people, and they mean no good to either of you. All that charm laid on last time you met them was a sham. They've decided they want you to fight for them — that's all it is.'

'Why are you telling us?' Dan asked bluntly. 'You're one of them.'

'Yes, but I'm not one of the Old Ones,' said Larch. 'Fir and I have a poor time of it with them; we're more like their servants than their friends. Me most, because I drop most of my leaves the way the summer people do.'

'I still don't see why they want us on their side all of a sudden,' said Daisy. 'Especially now Oak and Ash are dead.'

'You have something they think can be used for them in war,' said Larch. 'Use your wits. It's not a word I would utter, even beside your fence. Remember, though, that even if you consent to fight for them, you are not safe from their ill-will. If they had their way and held the dominions all year long, and winter ruled the world, they would turn

96

against the human race in any way they could.'

'Do you mean,' said Dan, 'that if they ever beat the summer Trees for good, winter would conquer summer?'

'Precisely,' said Larch. 'No sign of spring till May, first snow in October. It happens in some parts of the world; it could happen here.'

'We won't fight for that,' said Daisy emphatically.

'Keep out of their way, then,' said Larch. 'Keep out of the Forest. I must get away from this Death now. Here you are.' She put the ball into Daisy's hand and walked smartly into the trees.

'Out of the Forest!' grumbled Dan as they went back to the garden. 'How can we?'

'We've got to,' said Daisy. 'I won't fight for Ivy. I'll never forget how she half-strangled me; and about Oak and Ash. I only wonder, Dan, what the point of it all is. Can the summer Trees put up any resistance without their leaders, even when spring comes?'

'I nearly asked Larch that,' said Dan. 'Then I thought I didn't really want to know the answer. Anyway, she's a winter Tree, when all's said and done.'

Margaret was led to comment, over the next few weeks, how stuffy Dan and Daisy had become: sitting over their homework or the television even at week-ends, hardly putting their noses out of doors.

Finally the Forest caught up with the children — but not until just before Christmas. It was a tradition in the Sturgess family that the children fetched holly and ivy from the woods, the day before the twins' real birthday on 22 December. Daisy and Dan could remember first going as five-year-olds with Douglas and Margaret, and carrying the bundles the older children cut. This year, it seemed, they were to go alone. They put it off and put it off until late in the afternoon of 21 December — a snowy day, which gave them some excuse.

There were already signs of the early dusk when Mrs Sturgess came into the sitting-room where the children and

97

Margaret and Jamie were roasting chestnuts. She smelled of mincemeat and was wiping her hands on her striped apron.

'Are you children going for the evergreens, or are you not?' she asked. It was an ultimatum.

'Not,' said Dan hopefully. 'It's snowing.'

'It's stopped,' said Margaret, unsympathetic.

'But it's almost dark!' Daisy protested.

'There's snowlight — that'll light you,' said Margaret, and Jamie added, 'Take a torch!'

'Come with us, Margie,' said Daisy, at her most pathetic. 'You're so good at finding the best bits, with berries on.'

'No dice,' said Margaret briskly. 'I'm only waiting for you to go out, then Jamie and I are going to decorate the tree.'

This was another tradition. The Christmas tree was decorated for the twins' birthday, and their small real-birthday presents hung on it; it was then kept hidden in the cupboard under the stairs until the birthday morning.

'Oh heck,' said Dan feelingly. 'Do we have to go?'

'We've never had your birthday without the evergreens,' said Mrs Sturgess. 'Or the tree. Get off with you, now. You've just got time.'

'Track suits — quick,' said Daisy to Dan on the stairs. 'I'm not setting foot in that forest in my jeans.'

'Protective clothing essential,' Dan quoted. 'I should have asked for wellies for tomorrow's prezzy. Mine are getting tight.'

The snow was not deep underfoot, and the twins found skittering through it vastly enjoyable.

'Aren't the bare trees beautiful!' said Daisy, beginning to forget her fears. 'Even more than when they have their leaves. You can see all their shapes.'

'They aren't totally bare, if you look,' said Dan. 'Beech has husks on it still, and Oak has a few leaves. Ash has huge clumps of keys.'

They were hardly into the Forest before they met their Headmaster, Mr Dibden, coming out. He had impressive

98

boots, a knapsack and an ash stick; and an ordnance survey map in his hand.

'Oh, hello,' he said affably. 'I've been looking at your High Forest. Mr Briggs showed me your stuff, you know. Having seen what you were on about, I find your theory interesting. There's certainly some ancient woodland there; sharp of you to have spotted it. You're out late.'

'We're going for some holly,' said Dan.

'And ivy,' added Daisy, staring at Mr Dibden. She had had no idea that he even knew who they were.

'If the two of you do any further research, let me see it,' said the Head casually. 'I'm interested in all the Forest, but the ancient woodland most of all. History and folklore.' He nodded goodbye and stumped off.

'Folklore!' said Dan to Daisy as soon as Mr Dibden was out of earshot. 'If only he knew!'

'Well, he doesn't,' said Daisy. 'And he isn't going to. Come on, Dan. Evergreens.'

But there was one more interruption to their quest. A moving figure among the trees startled them to a shocked standstill.

'Winter people!' Dan muttered, grabbing Daisy. But it was Bramble who came out from a hazel thicket, barefoot but unshivering — and leaving no prints in the thin snow.

'Bramble!' exclaimed Daisy. 'What are you doing here? We thought all the summer people would be gone — resting inside their trees.'

'Storing their energies and all that,' said Dan. 'We haven't seen anybody else.'

'Don't come too close,' said Bramble. 'There's something in your pocket, isn't there? I'm about the only one of us around, as late as this. You see why, of course.'

The children didn't.

'Use your eyes,' said Bramble, slightly offended. 'Have you ever, even in midwinter, seen a bramble-bush bare of leaves? Of course not. Although I'm a leaf-stripper, I'm never leaf-less. Look!'

99

They looked to where he was pointing, and saw what he meant: a bramble-brake showed thick with leaves — a faded green marked with brown spots and edges.

'So I'm around, much of the winter,' said Bramble. 'I'm not one of the winter folk, but I don't rest much. Are you going to the celebration?'

'What celebration?' said Dan warily.

'The Turning,' said Bramble. 'Winter solstice. Midnight tonight. They start the party early, as the daylight is so short; they'll be beginning in an hour or less.'

'It's all celebrations!' said Daisy. 'Your Festivals, two Turnings, one — what do you call the November one?'

'The Changes,' said Bramble. 'Two Changes. It's what life's for, the celebrations.'

'Well, we aren't going to *theirs*,' said Dan roughly.

'Sh!' said Bramble. 'They're not far away. If you're staying, empty your pockets. If not, hurry home. The owls are out.'

He raced away, sliding over the snow-surface. The twins heard owls, hooting not far away.

'Come on, concentrate,' said Dan. 'Evergreens, you said.'

'In the next clearing,' said Daisy. 'I remember hollies there, and there's ivy everywhere.'

In the holly grove, the children cautiously fetched out the kitchen scissors (Daisy) and a high-class clasp knife with five blades (Dan). They weren't sure what reaction the metal might provoke; but there appeared to be none, and their bundles of holly and ivy grew big. At last they put down their tools and torch (hopefully hidden from winter eyes inside Daisy's muffler) and attended to the tying-up process.

'Wish there was mistletoe,' said Dan. 'I've never seen it, except up in the High Forest.' He struggled with a sprawling pile of twigs and a length of hairy twine. 'Put your hand or your foot or something on this, Daise,' he said, grappling, 'while I do a proper knot.'

A foot came down on his bundle and the wayward string: but it wasn't Daisy's foot. It was large, long, smooth and very

100

brown; and shoeless. Dan's head jerked up: he was looking at a sharp-eyed winter person.

'Daisy!' he shouted, jumping to his feet. 'Quick! Run for it!'

Too late, however: Daisy, as she turned towards him, turned into the grip of another winter Tree.

'Why the alarm?' said Dan's captor. 'You know me, surely; I'm Yew. You've seen me before. We're all friends here. Aren't we?' The words were warm, but there was a hint of menace about the tone.

'I'm Juniper,' said his companion. He was younger than the rather stern-looking Yew, and looked lively. 'We're messengers of the king and queen, come to invite you to the Turning feast. You'll come, of course?'

'Of course,' said Yew, underlining the force of the invitation. 'It was considerate of you to put aside your metal, and muffle it up, to allow us to approach you.'

'If we hadn't, could you just have touched us and said "Out iron, in wood"?' asked Daisy. 'Oak and Ash did.'

Juniper's grip on her grew tighter. 'Holders of dominions can do what others can't,' he said. 'March, now!'

'Here we go again,' Dan said to Daisy as they trudged towards the gathering-floor and the fire-stone. 'Does this remind you of anything?'

'We must try to get away,' Daisy whispered. 'Watch for a chance.'

This time they didn't have to traipse all the way. Where the upward slopes which led to the High Forest began, they met Ivy, walking lightly with a whitewood pitcher in her hand, her pale eyes shining in the dusk. She was wearing, Daisy noticed, Ash's ear-ring and ring.

'Are you coming to our feast?' she said in her sweet, husky voice. 'Good! I'm taking up the leafy dew from our hall. Guests are what we need to make the feast perfect. But you're worn out: let the wind take us.'

And their climb ended with a wild, brief ride in the spark-

101

ling cold of the rushing, frosty air, and a thump down into the untrampled snow where the winter people were already gathering round the ash-strewn stone, bringing twigs and branches to heap there.

'How will they light it?' Daisy whispered to Dan. 'Oak's and Ash's matches were burnt with their bodies; and the fire-cross is lost.'

'The slow way. Scouts' way,' said Dan. By mistake, he had a box of matches in his pocket, used to light his father's bonfire last week-end. But he meant to keep quiet about that. Dan might say little about his feeling for Oak, but he remembered it.

'Now our guests are here,' said Holly, smiling a welcome at the children, 'fire-building can stop and games can begin. Gather together, all my Trees!'

The winter people gathered round, exuberant, laughing and jostling.

'There are more here than there were at the November party,' said Dan to Holly. 'Have your numbers grown?'

'I've invited others besides the true foresters,' said Holly lightly. 'I don't see any need to stick to Oak's rigid rules about that, any more than to follow his system of excluding all but the Old Ones. Those days are past.' As he spoke he fingered the king's pebble pendant which hung round his neck. 'Most of the winter people are newcomers and outlanders anyway, so why fuss? Fir is here, and Larch and Spruce — besides Gorse and Privet, Box and Broom.' He pointed them all out.

'And Mistletoe,' said Dan, scowling.

'Of course,' said Holly, not sensing Dan's resentment of Mistletoe's behaviour. 'He is at all the feasts. And now,' he shouted, 'let the games start! Holly and his men, together — for "Hunt-the-Wren".'

'Why hunt the wren?' said Daisy to Ivy in bewilderment, as the Trees bustled into place.

'It's a game,' said Ivy. 'But it's a game about something

102

serious. The wren is my special bird, as you know. The king and his men hunted it in earnest once, when there was rivalry between Holly and me for the winter dominions. A lot of our games are about that time, though Holly and I live peacefully now.'

'Hunt-the-Wren' was a complicated game of chain-he in which the 'boys' did all the chasing and the 'girls' all the running away. Daisy and Dan, reluctant to start, found they enjoyed every minute of this.

After that there was a sort of musical trees, also much enjoyed by the twins. Dan realized that the only childish thing about many children's games was that it was children who played them. As interpreted by a gang of powerful, pushy Trees out for rough fun, these simple games took on an unimagined gusto.

'I like the winter people's parties better than the summer ones,' he admitted to Daisy as the noise and excitement mounted. 'Oak and Ash didn't have all these games.'

Daisy felt this was disloyal, but had no time to argue. Even she had lost her sense of being in real danger here.

As the dark gathered, torches (resinous branches of wood) were lit by Holly and Ivy, surrounded by a huddle of laughing winter people so that Daisy and Dan couldn't see how it was done. 'Have they got matches, after all?' Daisy whispered to Dan. He shook his head, puzzled.

'Another game,' called Ivy, as the torches were placed to light the clearing. 'This time — "Nay, Ivy, nay".'

The winter people shouted their enthusiasm. This game was evidently special.

It was another game of male-female rivalry, and it was played to a joking song sung by Holly and his side, which began,

> Nay, Ivy, nay,
> It shall not be, iwis,
> Let Holly have the maistry
> As the manner is.

The game was played rather like 'Oranges and Lemons', with the players choosing Holly or Ivy and forming up on either side for an eventual tug-of-war.

The twins conventionally chose their own sex, and Daisy found herself clasping Ivy's waist in the line-up for the tug-of-war. Bitterly, she noticed the butterfly-wing ear-ring gleaming in the light of one of the torches.

The tug-of-war was won by Ivy and her team: there was a sudden cave-in when all Holly's team crashed head first into Ivy's, and Dan was buffeted between heavy Tree bodies. Most of Ivy's side went over backwards, and Daisy rolled sideways to avoid being crushed in the mêlée. As she rolled, she saw that the ear-ring was now loose in Ivy's hair; and with no other thought than that of doing something to annoy Oak's murderers, she shot out a hand for it. Unnoticed, it went into her duffel-coat pocket, with a crumpled handkerchief and some very old bus tickets and a fluffed and battered humbug.

After the game, the Trees cooled off (emotionally speaking — they didn't suffer from actual heat or cold, and sat unconcerned in the snow) while songs were sung and music played. The children had a dryish log to sit on, and Daisy shuffled up to Dan.

'As soon as we get a chance, we must get away,' she whispered.

'Why now? It's quite fun,' Dan whispered back.

'I can't say here — but we've got to,' Daisy insisted. 'Really, Dan.'

'O.K.,' said Dan briefly. 'Next game.'

The next game was perfect for their purpose: it was a sort of 'Blind-man's-buff' and was played not only in the clearing, but in the surrounding trees. As the excitement grew, the children took their chance. As quietly as they could, in the snow and the softness of fallen leaves, they headed away from the gathering-floor and down the hill towards home.

After a quarter of an hour or so of near-silent scurrying, they stopped to get breath and to listen attentively to the

104

noises of the woods. Owls were calling, and a flock of small birds was on the move, making for the deepest cover; somewhere far off a fox barked. And then, near at hand, they heard a stealthy rustling in the bushes.

'Quick, Dan — they're after us,' said Daisy. She took to her heels, and Dan came thundering behind her. But his thundering came to an abrupt halt when a tree root caught his right foot on a steep bit of slope, and he pitched forwards for some distance and came down with a jarring crash. His left foot was bent back under his body weight. Daisy heard him fall, and turned back: to find him sitting huddled up, nursing his left wellington in both hands. Not far behind him, a startled badger — no doubt the maker of the rustlings — was scuttling to its set among the dark beech-trees.

'My ankle's busted,' Dan said through locked teeth.

—— 13 ——

Daisy was torn between concern for Dan and her urge to get away.

'It can't really be broken,' she said, kneeling down by him and staring at Dan's humped shape in the half-light.

'It thumping well is,' said Dan.

'Then we've had it,' said Daisy. Her gloved fingers momentarily touched the ear-ring in her pocket. What would Holly and Ivy do to a jewel-thief? 'All right, Dan. I'll get your boot off and we can see how bad it is.'

Trying to recollect last year's First Aid lectures, Daisy tugged off the boot and felt the ankle, to an accompaniment of bad language and occasional laughter from Dan.

'It's not broken,' said Daisy, gently massaging Dan's sock. 'It must be a sprain.'

'Give over,' snorted Dan, 'you're tickling. That's adding insult to injury. Anyway, I can't walk on it, Daise.'

'Try,' suggested Daisy hopefully. Dan did, but it was

105

clearly no good. The ankle was already swelling hugely. He stood on one foot in the snow, looking woebegone.

'I could make a crutch —' began Daisy.

'Oh, yes?' said Dan, driven to sarcasm by pain and frustration. 'With your bare hands? Don't be daft. There's only one thing to do — you must go back to the winter people, and get them to help.'

'No,' said Daisy vehemently. 'I won't.' She thought of the ear-ring and the dominion of air. Could she use it? Without revealing to Holly and Ivy that she had it?

'If we had a pony here,' she said to Dan, 'it could carry you home. I could help you up on it.'

'We haven't, as far as I can see,' said Dan bitterly, propping himself against a sweet chestnut tree. 'Anyway, I can't ride. Have some sense, Daise.'

'You don't have to ride — you just have to sit on it,' said Daisy. 'Shut up. I'm going to try.'

She pulled off her gloves, tucked them into a pocket and clasped the ear-ring between her bare hands.

'Queen's beasts, listen,' she said to the now silent woods. 'You know who I am, and how I fought for Ash all summer. Now I need help. One of you come and carry my brother.'

She slid the ear-ring back into safety, and stood listening.

'What good will that do?' said Dan, openly contemptuous. 'The wild ponies are miles away — probably out on the hills. Anyway, they won't come. Ivy's in charge, and they know you aren't Ivy.'

'Listen, Dan — listen,' said Daisy urgently. The hoof-falls of a four-footed animal — a sizeable animal walking lightly — could be heard. The moon was clear of clouds now and there was a sheet of pale light on the snow.

Between the trees, towards the children, came walking a full-grown stag. Its antlered head held high, it trod delicately, staring at them with an intense gaze. It came up close to Daisy and briefly lowered its head.

Dan flattened himself against the chestnut tree as the stag approached.

'Good grief, Daisy, what is it?' he said — the shadows of the trees still partly hiding it from him.

'Your transport,' said Daisy, and laughed. 'I meant to send for a pony, but I suppose the deer heard.' She realized that for Dan's sake she must pretend a confidence she was far from feeling.

'But I can't ride that!' said Dan blankly.

'Of course you can,' said Daisy, very brisk. She went up to the stag and rested her hand on its neck. It made a coughing noise in its throat. It sounded friendly enough.

'Come to my brother, queen's beast,' said Daisy. The stag accompanied her to Dan's tree.

'It can't really understand you,' said Dan, bewildered.

'It knows roughly what I mean,' said Daisy. 'Somehow it knows. I'll give you a leg up, Dan.'

Something of her apparent calm got into Dan. He accepted a leg up and perched on the stag's back, holding its neck with both hands.

'It's darned uncomfortable,' he said. 'Its backbone sticks out.'

'Don't grumble,' said Daisy. 'It's not a state coach, it's an ambulance.'

She glanced over her shoulder. Had she heard distant voices? The winter people might well be setting out in pursuit of them by now, having discovered the loss of Ivy's ear-ring. Led of course by Mistletoe — who could see better at night than by daylight.

'Walk on, stag,' she said firmly, as if to a recalcitrant pony. 'Home. To Fosters.'

'Is it supposed to know where we live?' asked Dan, hanging on grimly.

'It had better,' said Daisy. 'I'm not leading it — it's leading me.'

This was true. Daisy's right hand on the stag's neck found comfort and support as she scrambled and slid beside it. Her left hand, unromantically, carried Dan's discarded wellington.

'Are they following us?' said Dan, catching the sound of a far-off shout.

'I think so,' said Daisy. 'Queen's beasts,' she called, 'queen's birds! Cross our path behind us and confuse them. Scuff our footprints up.'

'Who do owls belong to?' said Dan, shivering.

'The winter people,' said Daisy. 'It came in one of their songs. Don't talk. Just ride.'

Dan's mount went surely and quickly. The evening was freezing now and the stag's breath steamed from its nostrils. Daisy looked at stars and moon and wondered how late it was, and when the Sturgess parents would begin to worry. Would they send police to look for the twins? With dogs? She imagined an encounter between stag and Alsatian, and grinned. Whose beasts were Alsatians? Could she call one off?

Dan worried more about the hunting owls. Were they only hunting? Or did they carry news of the children's progress to the winter people? He imagined being dive-bombed by an owl as he rode, and pulled the hood of his duffel-coat up.

In spite of the stag's speed, it seemed a long journey. They were not far off the last beech ride and the safety of home when they heard a human voice ahead. 'Dan! Daisy!' it called clearly. Surely it was Dad?

'Dare we shout back?' said Dan, thrilled but firmly keeping his head. 'Will it scare the stag?'

'It might,' said Daisy. 'Don't shout yet. Queen's beast, take us where our father is.'

The stag changed direction and went on unperturbed. More calling was heard, the light of torches seen, and the stag came out into the clearing where Dan and Daisy had left their evergreens and their edged tools. Bending over the abandoned greenery were Mr Sturgess, Margaret and Jamie. Mr Sturgess heard the stag first, straightened up, went stiff and said, 'God in heaven!' in a shaken voice.

'The dominion of air,' thought Daisy. 'Don't disturb the deer, Dad,' she said in her normal tone. 'It's friendly, but it

108

isn't tame. Dan's sprained his ankle and the deer will take us home.'

'Deer! It's a stag — a monster!' said Jamie.

'Are you sure it's safe?' asked Mr Sturgess. He was taken aback not only by the appearance of the stag but by finding his daughter, thirteen tomorrow, calmly in command of these odd events.

'Of course — we've come miles,' said Dan. 'It's agony to ride, though. Its backbone's like a bicycle-chain.

'Follow along behind us,' ordered Daisy. 'Don't crowd the stag. Are you bringing the green stuff? There's Mum's scissors and Dan's knife there somewhere. And a torch.'

'She's practising to be Prime Minister,' said Jamie loudly.

'She's not. She's Acting Queen,' said Dan, and giggled.

It was as well that Mrs Sturgess didn't get to the garden gate in time to see Dan slide off the stag, helped by Daisy, and the stag throw up its head and bound away.

'Thank you! Thank you!' Daisy called after it. 'Come here for food when the frost's bad. We'll leave you something at the gate.'

Dad and Jamie chaired Dan up the path, and Mrs Sturgess — in a flurry of relief — met them at the front door.

'Dan! What have you done?' she called out before they got him in.

'Only a sprained ankle, Mum,' said Daisy. 'It happened miles away, which is why we're so late.'

'Why did you go so far?' asked Margaret, idly curious. 'You'd got plenty of holly.'

'Oh — well, we went up to the High Forest. There's mistletoe there,' said Daisy evasively.

'Who wants mistletoe?' said Jamie, clasping Margaret's waist.

'What I want,' said Dan, 'is soup. And possibly crumpets. And golden syrup sandwiches. And cheese.'

'All at once,' added Daisy hopefully.

'I'll get the doctor,' said Mrs Sturgess, paying no attention to any of this. 'He ought to see that foot.'

109

'Then I'm going for a bath,' said Daisy, battling with her wellingtons. 'Food afterwards.'

When she came down again she found Dan in pyjamas and dressing-gown by the fire, his foot neatly bandaged. Her mother looked at her oddly, and Daisy guessed the story of the deer had been told.

'Don't fuss, Mum,' she said, giving her a hug. 'It was a friendly deer. It came up to us.'

'Oh well, obviously,' said Mrs Sturgess. 'It had probably been fed by people when it was a calf. All the same, it was a risk, Daisy.'

'I knew that,' said Daisy. 'I had to get Dan home. It was jolly cold, Mum. People die of the cold.'

'Exposure,' said Mrs Sturgess. 'You did well, Daisy. I'm not arguing.'

'One thing, though,' said Daisy casually. 'From my birthday, I'm going to be called Diana. Daisy's a baby's name, all small and cuddly. I think I'd rather be Diana now.'

'Queen and huntress, chaste and fair,' said Mr Sturgess, eating a crumpet. He had butter on his chin.

'What's that?' asked Daisy sharply.

'A poem. "Hymn to Diana",' said Mr Sturgess. 'Does it sound like you?'

Daisy punched him affectionately. She thought it sounded very like Ash.

'It's no good thinking we can start tomorrow,' said Mrs Sturgess. 'You'll have to give us time to get used to the idea. Give us till your official birthday and change your name then. We'll practise in the meantime.'

Daisy agreed, but Dan was discontented. 'It isn't fair,' he moaned. 'I want to change my name too, and now it sounds like copying. I don't like "Dan" much — all those playground rhymes! I wish you'd given me a real name, though. Not just an anagram.'

'But Aidan is a real name,' said Mr Sturgess, staring. 'We wouldn't inflict a made-up name on any of our children. It's a

110

Celtic name; there was a bishop called that, and he has a statue in Lindisfarne.'

'It's got a meaning,' said Mrs Sturgess. 'It means fire.'

'Fire!' said Dan, violently surprised. He slopped half of the soup in his mug over his knees and had to be mopped with a dishcloth.

Later that night, Daisy went into Dan's safely curtained room with a tin, which had had chemist's cough sweets in it, in her hand.

'I came to say good-night,' she said. 'And to show you this.'

She opened the tin, and showed Dan the single ear-ring, lying on a folded handkerchief.

'Daise!' exclaimed Dan, sitting bolt upright in bed. 'When did you get it? Was that why we had to get away?'

'When we played "Nay, Ivy, nay",' said Daisy. 'It fell off Ivy's ear, and I picked it out of her hair. Nobody saw me. But I think they'll guess, when they can't find it anywhere.'

'So that's why the stag came!' said Dan. 'It's marvellous! It's the air one, isn't it? Why didn't you get the wind to carry us?'

'I don't want the winter people to know for sure we've got it,' said Daisy. 'I think the box is Tree-proof, don't you?'

'What are you planning?' said Dan, eagerly. 'Can we fight the winter people? For the sake of Oak and Ash?'

'I sort of thought we might,' said Daisy. 'I don't see how. But we can be ready.'

She hid the little tin inside the larger metal box that held her sewing things, feeling that perhaps scissors and pins and needles were an added deterrent to Trees.

'A suit of armour would be the thing,' she told herself, falling asleep.

—— 14 ——

That night was too bitter for snow. The river froze, and the Forest birds and beasts huddled into themselves, fighting the cold. But next day the children woke to snow. It fell every day until Christmas: huge, steady flakes, which blanketed the ground and frilled leaves and branches. It froze most nights, and sliding, skating and snowballing filled children's days. It was hard on Dan, who could only hobble. Douglas (home for Christmas) and Jamie towed him about on a toboggan, but Mrs Sturgess vetoed real toboggan-rides for him.

'*And* I shan't be able to play football when school starts,' said Dan morosely.

Being less out-of-doors active than usual, he thought the more. Daisy, coming in early from a snowballing party because snow had got down her neck and into her boots, and her trailing hair was soaked, found him brooding by the fire.

'Come and talk,' he said, brightening up. 'Everybody's out, and I've been thinking. Diana, we ought to have done more to warn Oak and Ash about the winter people's plot.'

'Well, I did try,' said Daisy. 'Ash didn't believe there was really anything going on, and Oak's death and Ash's death didn't seem to surprise the summer people. Are you certain there's an actual plot? It's only what Mistletoe said. Larch talked about their wanting to use us in a war, but I didn't understand.'

'Yes, there is,' said Dan. 'Look, Diana — where's fire?'

'Lost,' said Daisy, combing out her hair.

'You said it was dirty work,' Dan reminded her. 'For both halves to be lost at the same time struck both Oak and Ash as too much of a coincidence. They couldn't believe each other. So suppose the two parts of the fire-cross were actually stolen?'

'Who by?' said Daisy. 'Holly? Ivy?'

'Keep guessing,' said Dan. 'Who goes everywhere? Who went freely in and out of both camps, all summer? Who is

112

always in the foreground at feasts and festivals, and could easily make a substitution — put an ordinary twig, say, where a fire-twig ought to be? Who sees in the dark — before the ritual fire is lit at midnight? Who's the spy? Who tried to buy our help?'

'Mistletoe,' said Daisy. 'Are we safe?'

'They won't come into the house,' said Dan. 'Touch wood!'

'No — that's their protection,' said Daisy. 'Touch metal. I don't want them to hear us, if they're about outside.'

She took up the poker from the hearth, and gave Dan the tongs. The children continued their discussion, solemnly holding fire-irons in front of their faces.

'And now I'm on to guessing,' said Dan. 'But I guess the winter people have got both halves of fire. Mistletoe could have stolen them at, or any time after, the spring festival, and given them to Holly or Ivy. They're keeping them hidden, waiting for the time to strike.'

'Why should they wait?' said Daisy. 'Why didn't they have their revolution last spring, if they had the fire-cross then?'

'They'd wait until they got the other dominions handed over to them,' said Dan.

'Oh, I see,' said Daisy. 'So when spring comes, you think they'll declare their revolution?'

'Something like that,' said Dan. 'And what's awful is that I feel that I've got to stop them. That only I can.'

'What's the point?' said Daisy sadly, and the poker drooped in her hands. 'Oak and Ash are dead.'

'It still matters,' said Dan doggedly. 'I'm still on their side. Aren't you? I bet you don't want seven months of winter every year.'

'But what can we do?' said Daisy. 'The summer people aren't here to help. You and I and Bramble can't fight the winter people all alone.'

'We may have to,' said Dan.

He had no chance to say more then — Mrs Sturgess came in

from work, and upbraided the children for sitting armed with the fire-irons and letting the fire go out.

But as the winter went on Daisy knew Dan was still fretting about the threat of the winter people.

It snowed on steadily — with short, inconclusive, useless thaws and more snow on top of them — into February, out of a nearly windless sky. At least Dan wasn't missing football — only indoor practices, as the pitches were unfit for play. But he became so frustrated by being cut off from sport that one mid-February Saturday he went for a forbidden afternoon of tobogganing with Terry and Jenk, was spilt and made the almost-recovered ankle bad again.

The following morning Daisy went to take him an elevenses mug of coffee and found him in his room, sitting on the edge of a homework-piled bed to look out of the window at the usual white vista.

'Turn your back to the window, and hang on to the mug — I brought an enamel one specially,' said Daisy, picking up a pair of compasses and holding it in front of her face. 'Aidan, I'm worried.'

'Well, we *are* twins,' said Dan. 'About fire, Diana —'

'No,' Daisy interrupted, 'I'm worried about me and air. I've got air. So I've got the wind.'

'Try gripewater!' said Dan with a shout of laughter.

'Grow up,' said Daisy. 'I'm in charge of the wind, Aidan. And for weeks, almost, it's gone on snowing, straight down. The clouds don't move, nothing moves. The weather forecast keeps saying that the weather-patterns of the Continent don't seem to be affecting England, and nobody understands why. Scotland and Wales had gale-force winds, which blew round most of the coast; but they just petered out inland.'

'Lordy!' said Dan. 'And you've got air shut up in a box.'

'Yes,' said Daisy. 'So I feel it's all my fault. My responsibility.'

'Like me and fire,' said Dan. 'I'm sure I've got to rescue it; that it's up to me.'

114

'I don't see how you can do it — you're dead lame. Unless you fight Holly single-handed, mounted on a stag,' said Daisy.

'Do you think you could find Bramble?' asked Dan, hopefully polite. 'Just to ask him what he knows about it all? I can't go far today. But if you could get him to come to the garage. . . .'

Daisy's heart sank into her slippers. To go alone into the Forest, even just inside the edge of it — into Holly and Ivy's domain — when perhaps they knew what she had done: how dare she?

'All right,' she said. 'Forward the Light Brigade!'

'You mean the fire brigade,' said Dan. 'Neither of the children managed a laugh.

Before she set out, Daisy made sure that the butterfly symbol of air was properly hidden. A tin inside a metal box: she couldn't do much more.

It was a thawing day, with a few moist flakes of snow settling on to a wettish surface; the air was harsh to breathe. Daisy stamped her feet and whistled along the lane, shirking the direct plunge into trees where the beech ride started. She lingered by the bramble thicket where she and Dan had met Mistletoe.

'I want Bramble,' she said to the Forest. 'Can somebody find Bramble?'

No answer: so she trudged on. It was a longish trudge. She saw Privet in the distance, but he paid no attention to her; she saw several groups of human beings, with sledges and cameras and dogs. Bramble suddenly appeared from behind one of these — a noisy snowball party — almost as if he were using them as a shield.

'Walk home with me,' Daisy whispered to him as soon as the human backs were turned.

'Follow the people down,' said Bramble. 'I think we're overlooked. Yew is about, and Privet.'

Fortunately for the success of this plan, the snowballers

115

went almost to the gates of Fosters. At the bend of the lane they turned towards the church and Daisy and Bramble turned off on the short Fosters track. Once inside the gate of home, Daisy gave a skip of relief.

'In here,' she whispered, pulling the garage door just wide enough open, and tugged Bramble in.

At once, Bramble shied violently back. 'No! No! No!' seemed to be all he could say; he shook from head to foot.

'Can't you bear it?' said Daisy, disconcerted. 'Mistletoe came in.'

'He's different,' gasped Bramble. 'Let me out! I can't stay.'

'Have some wood to touch,' said Daisy. She put the handle of the garden broom into his hand: at once Bramble became calmer. His teeth still chattered, but he seemed in control of himself. All the same, he jumped in alarm when Dan sidled in; and he backed up against one of the wooden uprights of the garage wall and leaned heavily against it.

Dan took in the situation. 'Will anyone hear us if we talk here, Bramble?' he asked. 'Where we stand?'

'I doubt whether anyone would come as close as this to — that,' said Bramble, indicating the car. 'Don't make me touch it!'

'All right,' said Dan. 'Have you found out anything about what's going on in the Forest? Are we right in thinking that Holly and Ivy are plotting something?'

'I've been told nothing,' said Bramble. 'But Holly and Ivy have their weapons in readiness. And from what I can see, they have some instant way of starting fire. That's all.'

'Ah,' said Dan. 'And what —'

'No!' Daisy interrupted him. 'We've had two questions. Oak said it was always three. And I want one.'

Dan stayed quiet, and Daisy phrased her question carefully.

'Is it because of Ivy, and the way she manages the dominion of air, that it keeps snowing?' she asked, deviously.

'Presumably,' said Bramble. 'Wind moves cloud about; cloud produces precipitation.'

116

'All over England?' said Daisy. 'That's the same question.'

'Of course, all England,' said Bramble. 'The Forest is Heartwood — didn't you know? Not Hartwood because of the deer in it; that's a new idea. But because, of all the great old forests, it's the one nearest to the middle of the kingdom. Who rules here, rules England. But not the Great West. Or the Great Winter.'

'Wales,' guessed Dan.

'And Scotland,' added Daisy.

'You must give me one more question,' said Dan pressingly. 'Who controls the sun?'

Even in his distressed state, Bramble laughed. It came out like a fox's bark.

'Nobody — of course,' he said. 'What fools you are! The sun is at the centre of the balance. It controls the dominions, not they it; and the balance controls it in its turn. Sun and moon, earth and water and fire and air — they are all dancing the dance of the balance, and so are we all.'

'It's too complicated,' Dan complained.

'You've got no wits for it,' said Bramble snappily. 'And now — let me go!'

They would have had a job to stop him. He shouldered his way to the door, and whizzed away down the little drive, jumping the gates like a hurdler.

'We're no further forward,' grumbled Dan.

'Yes we are,' said Daisy. 'Get in the car. I've thought of something.'

Dan expressed a mock amazement; but he got in the car, and the children conferred.

'From what Bramble said, everything seems all knotted up together in this balance,' said Daisy. 'The dominions, and the sun and moon, and the weather. So air must know where fire is. Suppose the symbol of air can tell us?'

'What, an ear-ring?' scoffed Dan. 'How?'

'Come up to my room after tea, when it's dark,' said Daisy. 'I want to try.'

117

After dark, the children crept into Daisy's room. They left the light off and made sure that the window — which opened on to the bare branches of the giant ash tree — was securely shut and curtained. Daisy held the ear-ring between her hands and Dan closed his hands around hers; two layers of human flesh and bone, to keep the symbol of air from the prying of any spies.

Daisy whispered into the crack of her folded hands, 'Air! Where is fire?'

At once the children turned, startled. The window was torn open and the curtains whirled aside. It was as if a storm of wind had struck the ash tree, but no other tree in the garden. Its branches tossed and rattled, and a murmuring sound came as they rubbed together. 'The s-stone!' it seemed to say, soft and sibilant. 'The s-stone!'

'Stop!' exclaimed Daisy, into her hands. Dan let her go and limped at his best speed to shut the window and curtains.

'My eye!' he said, as the freak wind died away. 'We do see life!'

Daisy shivered, and slid the ear-ring back into its box.

'Does it help?' she said. 'What stone? The Forest's full of stones.'

'Oh yes, it helps,' said Dan, picking up a knitting-needle. 'There's only one stone, for dominions and for Trees: *the* stone, the fire-stone. Of course, that's where they'd hide it; nearest to where they use it. Under the stone. Oak or Ash wouldn't move that stone; it's too special to them.'

'Dare we go there — with the Forest full of winter Trees out to get us?' asked Daisy.

'We must,' said Dan. 'As soon as I can walk that far. And as soon as I've thought how we can manage it without being seen. I don't want to be shot at by Holly, any more than you want to be choked by Ivy.'

It was the end of February before they went. By then Dan felt up to the walk; but he was still slow.

Since Daisy had briefly stirred up air, there seemed more

118

wind about, though the weather was mainly frosty now, with clear skies and sparkling days. The snow was crisp and crusty as icing, and creaked and crumped under the children's boots (Dan had his father's gumboots, to allow some room for the bandage he still wore). Their slightly uncertain progress to the gathering-floor — they were still not entirely sure of the way, and made some unnecessary detours — took them two or three hours one Saturday. Dan took a tough walking-stick to help him along, but Daisy had her hands cupped against her chest, enclosing something inside them.

'If teeth protect fillings, perhaps hands will protect what we need,' Dan had argued. 'How else are we to take metal through the Forest? Undetected?'

There must have been winter people around; but winter people excelled at lying low, and they did not appear. It seemed that nobody was taking any interest in what the children did. They once thought they saw Hazel slipping between two tree-trunks, and were puzzled. They saw a robin too, and several times a wren; and wondered how close the winter king and queen might be.

The gathering-floor lay snow-covered, with the imprints of bird-feet and rabbit-feet criss-crossing all over it. The stone looked white and innocent.

'Suppose we're wrong,' Dan muttered.

'We aren't,' said Daisy. 'Rest your foot. I'll do it. Here — hold the end.'

She gave Dan one end of a coil of slender, flexible wire, and as quickly as she could she went around the trees surrounding the clearing, looping the wire around each one to make a belt as high as her elbows until the gathering-floor was completely encircled by a metal band. When she got back to Dan she twisted wire around wire to complete the circuit and let the rest of the coil fall into the snow which made deep pockets between the beech-tree roots.

The stone, the clearing and the children were fast inside the wire ring. Dan sighed with excitement.

119

'So far so good,' he said. 'Oh, Diana — I hope it works. It looks so thin. I hope they really can't see and hear us while we're inside.'

'It's got to work,' said Daisy. 'Queen's birds! Queen's beasts! Out of the ring.'

'You haven't got you-know-what,' said Dan.

'I don't think I have to, now they know me,' said Daisy; and with a whirr and a rustle, a scattering of small birds flew up out of the surrounding trees.

'Out, all birds of the air,' said Daisy, thinking of the king's. She clapped her hands to reinforce the order.

'We needn't worry about animals,' said Dan. 'There won't be any within miles, after you've racketed around.'

'Thanks so much,' said Daisy. 'Who owns woodlice?'

'Suppose we can't lift it!' said Dan, his eyes on the fire-stone. 'It's huge.'

'Use your stick as a lever,' said Daisy. 'You're the one who's good at mechanical things! I'll roll a smaller stone close.'

Sparked with enthusiasm, Dan did as she said. It was a simple lever, but effective. The tough ash walking-stick held, one end of the great stone moved up, and Daisy scrabbled briefly underneath.

'Do you think this is it?' she said, shaking off her hands muddy fragments of soil and showing Dan her find. Two slender pieces of barkless branch, one of which was of a size to fit into a hole which pierced the other.

'That's it,' said Dan, taking the two from her. 'You rub the inside one to and fro, and the friction makes —'

As he spoke he slid one piece of wood into the other: fire sprang under his hands, and he jerked them rapidly apart again.

'Usually, it takes ages,' he said. 'So this must be the right thing. It's quite small. It would be easy to sneak off with it during one of the Tree festivals.'

'Hide it,' said Daisy. 'And I'll take the wire down.'

120

'I vote we leave the wire,' said Dan. 'See, if the winter people can't get in they won't know the fire symbols have gone. And they won't see our footprints, if the floor is enclosed with metal.'

With the fire-cross deep in his pocket, he ducked awkwardly under the wire. Daisy handed him his stick and followed more nimbly.

'Home,' she said with satisfaction. 'And fast; I'm starving.'

'Fast is what it won't be,' said Dan. 'I've walked too far on this foot already. I'll have to dot-and-carry-one back.'

Daisy linked her arm in his for moral support, and they trekked in silence for a while. The quiet of the winter woods seemed to close around them like a bell of glass. 'Shake the world, and it'll come down a snowstorm,' Daisy thought, timing her steps to Dan's increasingly dragging gait.

But the stillness was not absolute. And as they struggled along first Daisy and then Dan became aware that others were travelling with them. Always just out of eyeshot, behind thickets or the boles of substantial trees, winter people were keeping pace with them on both sides.

—— 15 ——

'I can't go any quicker,' Dan muttered to Daisy, unable to hide his alarm.

'Just keep going,' said Daisy doggedly. 'They don't seem to be closing in.'

'They are a bit I think,' said Dan.

'They're the same distance away; they're just being less cautious about showing themselves,' said Daisy. 'I wonder what they're up to — whether they know we've got what we've got.'

'They can't do,' said Dan, but his frown of effort became even more of a scowl.

121

He lumbered on for a while, looking only at the ground under his feet. It was Daisy whose anxious peering picked out Holly's figure, and then Yew's, among their fellow-travellers.

They were hardly out of the High Forest when Dan stumbled, skidded a few steps, and came to a stop.

'I don't think I can do it,' he whispered to Daisy. 'I've really done this foot in; it hurts like hell. I'll just have to stop somewhere and give it a rest. You head for home: at least they won't have got us both.'

'Don't be daft,' said Daisy. 'I wonder if a summer tree would protect us at all?'

'What on earth do you mean?' said Dan.

'The Hermit's Oak,' said Daisy. 'It isn't far away. Could you get that far? We could get inside it and you could rest. Maybe an oak would be a deterrent.'

'Come on, then,' said Dan. 'It's got to be somewhere. Give it a try.'

The Hermit's Oak was a huge tree on the borders of High Forest and Low Woods, split by a fissure which ran three metres up the trunk, and hollow at its base. Local story said that it was five hundred years old and that a holy hermit had once used it for his cell; but Mr Briggs insisted that the hermit had lived in a hut by the church, where he could beg from church-goers, and that the legend was unverisimilitudinous fictification and all his eye.

The twins knew from past experience that two skinny people could fit inside the tree, standing up. Dan crawled in first and straightened himself and his stick; Daisy crept after him and put her face to the fissure to watch events. She got no reassurance from seeing the winter people slide out of their cover and move up to encircle the tree.

'What are they doing?' muttered Dan.

'Standing around us,' said Daisy. 'Now they're talking to each other.'

'No — listen,' said Dan. 'They're talking to us.'

'Talking' was one way of describing it. What the winter

122

Trees did was to whisper, in low sibilant words which were perfectly audible inside the oak — the woods were so still. Normal talking from Holly and Ivy would have been bad enough; the throaty murmur that came from them and their comrades was far more sinister. Dan and Daisy hated it, and their skins grew gooseflesh as they had to hear.

'Do you suppose you are protected?' Holly whispered first. 'That the wood of the oak will do anything for you? Think again. You saw Oak die and Ash die. Their people are asleep.'

'Except for Hazel and Bramble — and even those have gone back now to their rest,' murmured Ivy. 'If they hadn't been around, we'd have had you sooner. Now you're ours, even with a little skin of oak to shell you in. Oak and Ash can do nothing for you now.'

'Don't answer,' Dan said softly to Daisy. 'Whatever they say. Don't answer.'

'All right,' said Daisy. 'Not much to say, anyway. Just 'No'. It's horrible listening to them, though.'

'Gruesome,' agreed Dan.

'Don't browbeat the dear children, Ivy, my love,' said Holly, going back to his earlier jolly tone. Combined with a guttural whisper the effect was downright nasty. 'We used threats before, and the dear things took no notice.'

'More fools they,' said Ivy.

'We should have been nicer, shouldn't we,' said Holly. 'Made it clear we want to be friends. We do want to be friends; don't we, Trees?'

'Yes, yes. Friends,' hissed the winter Trees all around. Daisy, her eye to the crack, caught sight of Larch in the circle; Larch seemed to be the only one of them who was silent. 'Good for Larch,' she thought.

'Get on with it, Holly,' said Ivy sharply.

'Don't rush me, dear heart,' said Holly in his sugary snarl. 'We've all the time in the world. The children are not going to leave us, are they? We've got all night.'

With dismay Daisy realized that the daylight was beginning to fail. The eyes of the winter people glittered bright in the low, late rays of the westering sun.

'What I had in mind, my darlings,' he went on, 'was a coalition between us. A sharing of power. You've been only vassals to Oak and Ash — now haven't you? Come here, go there, do this, don't do that, and reprimands for stepping out of line in any way.'

'That's true, whether we like it or not,' Dan said to Daisy.

'Poor things. What a life!' murmured Yew.

'Shocking,' said another voice, that Daisy thought came from Juniper.

'That's not our way at all,' Holly went on. 'We'd offer you a share in everything, including the power.'

'You realize what we want for our part,' Ivy's voice interrupted. 'We want the control of the dominions all the year round — no more of yielding them up in the stinking spring; no more of skulking in our trees in the summer months, or lying low in our hall, while the summer lords and their toadies flaunt around our woodlands in the heat and dance at our sacred fire.'

'Babbling on about the balance,' added Holly, the honey momentarily gone from his voice. 'Of course there must be balance: but balance means extremes. You balance a seesaw by weighting the ends, not by getting in a huddle in the middle. How can we play our part when our end has so little weight?'

'Help us to the power, and we'll do the balancing all right!' exclaimed Ivy. 'We'll balance the trees in the woods, winter against summer. More of us, fewer of them. We've never had our chance: in the past the summer trees have ruled this country. So balance demands we rule it for a time, and our folk stock the woods.'

'How you do carry on Ivy,' said Holly. 'Don't make the dear children think we're out for genocide. Just a little quiet justice for a change.'

124

'And the seasons,' Ivy interrupted. 'We redress the balance there, too. There's been too much battering sun and shattering light altogether. Nine months winter in a year could hardly be too long. Why not more, indeed? Winter all year.'

'Now dears,' said Holly, the insidious whisper pouring on. 'How about King Aidan and Queen Diana for part of the year? Like the sound of it, do you? So do we. We could have good times together. Don't you agree?'

Daisy drew an exasperated breath for a biting reply, but 'Sh!' Dan said before she could utter it. 'Don't argue. We know they're liars. No point in saying so.'

'They're not answering,' said somebody out of Daisy's range of vision — maybe Fir or Pine.

'Then we're on a wrong tack with them,' came Ivy's vicious whisper. 'Give me a go at them. Move in.'

The whole circle of winter Trees closed in a little, and Daisy shivered inside the cleft in the oak.

'Now, listen,' said Ivy, low but sharp. 'We've made you an offer. You know what we want. We want you to use what you have on our behalf, as you have done for Oak and Ash. The unspeakable thing. The Death.'

'Metal!' exclaimed Daisy to Dan. 'So that's what they're on about.'

'We ought to have guessed,' said Dan. 'It makes sense of all this carry-on.'

'We don't ask much,' said Ivy. 'A little Death to seal off Oak's and Ash's halls so that they can't rearm. Death in your hands when they advance to attack us — the Death that leaps across a hillside, spitting noise and fire.'

'Guns!' exclaimed Dan. 'We can't get guns. We're children.'

'Oh — and why not?' said Ivy. 'You got fire. If you held *that* Death, Oak and Ash would never dare to come near us — the war would be a walk-over. Not a single casualty — think how many lives you would save. And end sharing power with us for ever after. What do you say?'

125

The children said nothing, but Dan shifted his weight uncomfortably on to his good foot.

The winter Trees moved in another step.

'So you despise our good offer,' said Ivy. 'Then hear the other side of things. Do you suppose, if you refuse us, you'll be safe in these woodlands ever again? In broad daylight ivy will trip you up and holly prickles scratch the sight out of your eyes. Branches will whip around your legs when you think you're on open paths, and you'll fall on stones and crack your shins till the bones stick through the skin. Great boughs will thump down on you when there's no wind stirring. And not only on you. Your sister, your parents, your friends. Nobody of yours will be safe if you stand out against us. Not only this winter, but every winter. While the summer lords lie quiet, we'll be at your backs.'

'Don't listen,' said Dan to Daisy. 'Stop your ears.'

Both children covered their ears with their hands and huddled together. They were increasingly cold and hungry, Dan's ankle throbbed under his weight, and light faded steadily outside their tree.

At last Daisy realized that the winter Trees had said their say: the insistent mutter of threats had died away and Holly, Ivy and their crew stood waiting, all eyes on the Hermit's Oak.

'They've stopped,' she whispered, pulling one of Dan's hands from an ear. 'But they're still watching and listening.'

'My ankle's agony,' said Dan. 'If only I could sit down! We're trapped, and it's getting late. It must be.'

'I'll squeeze right back against the tree — see if there's room for you to sit,' said Daisy. She squirmed back against the trunk, forcing herself not to think of spiders; but there was still no room for Dan to bend his knees in comfort.

'No good,' he said grimly. 'What else can we try?'

'We could yell, but there's nobody about,' said Daisy.

'What about fire?' said Dan, whispering even more softly. 'Can we use that? You used air to bring the deer. We've got fire, this time.'

126

'That's an idea,' said Daisy. 'But we mustn't speak aloud. Perhaps something will hear us if we whisper.'

'Creepy-crawlies,' said Dan. 'They can't do much. I'd say there were bats in this tree, but they'll be hibernating.'

Daisy shuddered, and shook herself slightly.

Wriggling to free an elbow, Dan drew the fire-cross cautiously out of his pocket and whispered, bending his face towards it so that it almost touched his lips.

'Fire — help us!' he said. 'King's beasts, queen's beasts, come and help us escape. We serve the balance. — Shift round,' he added to Daisy, but still under his breath. 'I want a go at looking out.'

He was alarmed, when he got his eye to the crack, to see how close the ring of winter people stood and how the dark was thickening.

His ears were nearer to the outside world, too, and so it was he who first heard sounds of disturbance in the wood around. He thought he caught running feet, and even human voices.

'People!' said Daisy joyfully, catching the sounds in her turn. Even as she spoke, the circle around the oak broke up and the winter people dispersed among the trees around, as quiet as shadows.

A dog-fox, coming at an easy run, loped past the oak and was gone into the nearest thicket. After it, air-guns in hand, came crashing Terry and Jenk, booted and hatted like a polar expedition and making as much noise as a school outing. The twins burst out of their hiding-place and shouted an ecstatic welcome.

'Oh heck!' said Jenk, not at all pleased to see them. 'We were after a fox — you'll have scared it to blazes.'

'*We* will!' exclaimed Dan, incensed. 'You were about as quiet as a goods train, yourselves. What are you at? You can't bag a fox with an air gun.'

'Who can't?' said Terry. 'Anyway what are you — Dan, Dan the dirty old hermit? What's the point of getting in a tree?'

'Nature project,' said Daisy coldly. 'Are you on foot, Terry?'

'Natch,' said Terry. 'I don't chance the bike over all this snow and muck.'

'I only ask because Dan's done his foot in,' said Daisy.

'Oh well, you're all right there,' said Terry. 'The Markham girls are out with their sledge — give a shout. They were squirrel-spotting some way back.'

'No need to shout,' said Jenk. 'They're here. Plus squirrel.'

He pointed where a grey squirrel shot, undulating, up a lime to its twiggy drey at the top. Monica and Patsy came panting into sight, laden with binoculars (Patsy) and towing a sleigh with metal runners (Monica). Daisy immediately bore down upon Monica and bargained for the loan of the sleigh.

'It's not much use — you can't go any speed up here,' said Monica. 'It's all tree-roots and rabbit-holes and upsidownsiness. Still, Dan can sit on it and rest his foot and you can pitch down the good bits. You're welcome. We want to watch the squirrel. Is it building already, or is it too early?

'Come with us,' Daisy suggested hopefully, thinking she would be glad of an escort. But Patsy and Monica were in no hurry to leave; another squirrel, in the Hermit's Oak itself, saw to that.

The twins set off alone, in some trepidation, but hoping the metal of the sleigh-runners might fend off Ivy and Holly. This was never necessary. Only three minutes' slide further on they met Margaret and Jamie, watching the behaviour of a flock of long-tailed tits as they headed for cover for the approaching night. Margaret fussed and scolded over Dan, and Jamie steered the sleigh to Fosters over the bumps and humps of the woodland tracks. No ivy tripped him, and no branches fell on anyone's head.

Daisy and Dan listened stoically to the anxious reproaches of both their parents, and made the best of a huge high tea, hot baths, and (for Dan) early bed. Daisy took her homework to his room, but it never got done.

'They did us proud, didn't they,' said Dan. 'A fox, two squirrels, and goodness knows how many tits.'

'And six people,' said Daisy. 'Whose beasts are we? We live above ground, but perhaps our ancestors lived down in caves.'

'Trees, more like,' said Dan. 'Queen's beasts.'

'Anyway it's a comfort that the animals heard and came,' said Daisy. 'Where's you-know-what?'

Dan whispered between the points of his compasses, 'Money-box — my cash-box one with a key — inside tin trunk I use for sports gear. All right, do you think?'

'Sounds it,' said Daisy. She sighed. 'But I can't feel sure it was a good day's work. Being trapped by the winter ones like that, and having to hear all that stuff. Promises, threats, growling. You can't believe the promises but you can jolly well believe the threats.'

'It's still good,' said Dan. 'It was something I had to do, and I've done it. We both did, I mean; it was half and half. We've got it.'

'Don't gloat yet,' said Daisy. 'We may have got it, but what — what are we going to do with it?'

'The question may be,' said Dan, 'what is it going to do with us?'

Spring

— 16 —

When the snow finally went, rain followed: weeks of cold, cloudy, heavy weather. Daisy bothered about it, and one day fetched air out of its box and whispered to it, 'I don't know what to do — but I feel sure it ought to be windier. Do what you think you ought.' This was followed by three days of gales; a lot of damage was done in the Forest and two green-gage trees in the Markhams' orchard were blown down. Daisy decided to leave things alone, and March went back to being uncharacteristically still and damp. People grumbled about the lateness of the spring.

On and off, Daisy and Dan put their minds to the Forest. They both, that term, acquired a reputation for being inattentive in class and for handing in scatty homework. Mr Briggs asked them privately if everything was all right at home; Margaret gave them a scolding about wasting the opportunities of youth.

'Opportunities of youth!' Dan snorted afterwards to Daisy. 'I don't feel young. I feel ninety. A rather elderly ninety. It's not being able to budge that's the trouble.'

'Well, we can't budge,' said Daisy, her tension showing in snappiness. 'Holly and Ivy seem to wear the earth and water badges most of the time, so we've no way I can think of of getting those. And you know we daren't set foot in the Forest now, anyway, for fear of what they'll do.'

But both twins felt that the next move was up to them themselves.

About the beginning of March, they began to notice that the winter people were often close to Fosters. The school bus got back in full daylight now, and as Dan and Daisy walked home they usually saw a tall figure in among the shadows of

133

the trees. Sometimes the watcher moved on a line parallel to the children's walk home; sometimes, it remained motionless, observing. At week-ends when Daisy and Dan were out in the garden, the winter people seemed to be about all day, on the edges of the Forest and even in the lane. They might give an appearance of being busy with concerns of their own; or they might just watch.

'We're prisoners in our own house,' said Dan. 'It must be like this, being under house-arrest.'

'They still want us,' said Daisy. 'I wonder if they've been inside the ring of wire. Mistletoe might dare to. Even if they haven't, they may have some way of knowing that fire isn't answerable to them any more.'

'If I were them, I'd suspect Mistletoe,' said Dan.

The children did debate whether to make a sortie into the Forest and see what happened, but decided that they couldn't risk it. If Holly or Ivy instantly took them prisoner, and dragged them away to the winter people's hall, it would be the end of their chances of being of active help to the summer people. 'And a bit hard on Mum and Dad,' added Dan thoughtfully.

The Easter holidays were exceptionally tiresome. The Forest was greening over and full of birdsong, and the winter people more vigilant than ever — around the house and garden from dawn until dusk. The twins, seriously frightened now and worried by daytime twitchiness and the night's bad dreams, only ventured among the trees with their parents, or Margaret and Jamie. Fortunately Jamie, finding the archery handbook still lying around, got interested in shooting, and borrowed bows for himself and Margaret from a friend in Melbury: so archery — which Mr Sturgess permitted if Jamie was in charge — was taken up again by the younger Sturgesses.

At the very end of April, on the day when school began again, Daisy and Dan noticed a new sign among the winter people. The watchers around Fosters were now carrying bows, and had quivers at their backs.

'Something's going to happen soon,' said Dan as soon as the children had got into the kitchen and arranged themselves on either side of — and leaning on — the gas-stove.

'It's bound to, isn't it,' said Daisy. 'The second of the Changes must be due; most of the trees are in leaf now. Funny that oak and ash are among the latest, when they're king and queen. I suppose the new king and queen will be an oak and an ash, and not beech and lime, or something?'

'It'll be oak and ash,' said Dan. This was something he felt positive about, among the mysteries. 'Diana, do you suppose — I wonder if the second Change is the first of May?'

'Would it always be the same day?' said Daisy doubtfully.

'I suppose it shouldn't be,' said Dan. 'But I'm thinking of the shared religion, and that people always went to the woods that day.'

'And had a May Queen and a Green Man,' said Daisy. 'They had to go at sunrise, Mr Briggs says.'

'Oh no,' said Dan. 'That's practically the middle of the night! How are we going to get out of the house without waking the family?'

'So we're going, are we?' said Daisy. 'All right, we're going! I didn't say we weren't.'

'I think we've got to,' said Dan. 'If we don't warn the summer people what's up, they'll walk into some trap of the winter Trees.'

'In that case,' said Daisy, 'we just make a statement. Why not?'

So it was that at supper that night, Daisy said casually to her mother, 'Mum — Aidan and I are going to the woods for breakfast on Friday, because it's May the first. Can we take our food? We'll do most of it the night before.'

'Hard-boiled eggs,' said Dan helpfully. 'And cold sausages.'

'Is this one of your Mr Briggs's ideas? He seems to be a history-nut,' said Mrs Sturgess. 'Who else is going?'

'Oh, lots of us,' said Daisy. 'It'll be fun. All madly traditional.'

135

'We never did this when I was in his form,' said Margaret. 'He's getting worse.'

'All right, you can go,' said Mrs Sturgess. 'But be back to get the bus — it's still a school day, May the first or not. What time do you have to be there?'

'Sunrise,' said Dan, and Mrs Sturgess exclaimed, 'What! That's about half-past five!'

'We won't wake you,' said Daisy. 'We'll creep.'

'Just don't come back if you forget anything,' said Mr Sturgess. 'That's all.'

Daisy and Dan did not forget anything. At about twenty past five they were standing on the Fosters lawn, fully equipped with track-suits, wellingtons (Dan had new ones), and duffel-coats, the capacious pockets of which held food and well-wrapped treasures. They were both armed. Dan held clasped right inside his folded fingers a small, one-bladed penknife; Daisy similarly held her tiny scissors, meant for embroidery. Daisy had put on the lawn a metal hoop, which had once been her grandfather's bowling hoop; both children stood huddled within the circle it made on the grass. They were cold with the earliness of the morning, their lack of breakfast, and a sickening apprehension.

There was nobody about. The light was still and grey and a few birds were chatting quietly; the dew lay heavy, marked only by the children's footprints. There was no movement anywhere to suggest the presence of the winter people.

Daisy's unarmed hand — her right — went into her pocket and she whispered, 'Air! Take us where we shall be safe — where Oak's and Ash's people are.'

With a whirl and a rush, they went up. Dan curled up his toes, anxious that his rather loose wellingtons should not fall off. The children remembered not to speak, but would have liked to shout and sing. They met a heron, long legs trailing out behind as it flew; but their speed took them past before they had time to enjoy the feeling of meeting birds on their own territory.

136

The air set them down in a green glade where were two people they knew: Silver Birch, skinny and golden-haired, and Hawthorn. Silver Birch was carrying a pitcher; Hawthorn's arms were full of his own fresh-gathered branches, where the mayflower was just showing white in the bud, framed by rich leaf.

'Hawthorn!' said Dan, overjoyed. 'You're awake!'

'Of course,' said Hawthorn. 'Up and out. It's the day. It's sunrise. And I have a message for you, young friend. The person who is asleep under that tree says you may wake him up. To restore a balance between you.'

Dan looked, and saw that the tree Hawthorn's nod was indicating was the very oak tree where he had slept last Midsummer Day. At its foot lay — what? A heap of branches and leaves?

The children raced towards it, Dan first. When he got there he stopped, fearfully. Did he dare to move the branches? He thought he saw among them a long, pale hand. He lifted away, one bough, and became sure: among the leaves was a sleeping face. Still and almost colourless, it was like a face of stone; it seemed as if the leaves grew out of it as they did out of the foliate head in the church.

'It's a dead body,' said Daisy behind his shoulder.

'Don't be daft,' said Dan, moving again. 'It's Oak.'

'Yes, but he's dead,' said Daisy.

'Watch,' said Dan. He dragged more branches off.

'He isn't breathing,' said Daisy.

'They don't,' said Dan. 'Not like us, I mean.'

'Don't touch him,' said Daisy — not afraid, but shrinking from the awesomeness.

'I have to wake him,' said Dan. He touched Oak's hand: it was cold. Dan reminded himself firmly that Oak's hands were always cold. He took the heavy shoulder and gave it an almighty shake.

Not little by little, but all in one movement, Oak woke and sat up. He rubbed his face, which began to show colour; he ran his hands through his curly hair. Bits of twig and leaf dropped out, and an earwig and a millipede or two.

'Thanks for your kind offices,' he said to Dan. 'So the oak is out before the ash?'

'How do you mean?' Dan asked.

'If the ash had been out first, the queen would have waked me,' said the king. 'As it is, I wake her. Come along.'

'King, I've got to warn you — ' began Dan.

'Not now — not now. None of that now,' said Oak impatiently. 'Tell me later. First things first.'

He got up, and clapped his hands. Silver Birch had gone, but the glade rapidly filled with Oak's men, all wide-awake and smiling.

'But weren't you really dead?' Daisy said urgently to Oak, as they watched the tree-people come.

'Of course I was,' said Oak. 'But at the same time, not dead. You are in the presence of one of the great mysteries. It can't be explained, though it can be understood.'

'Well, I don't understand it,' complained Daisy.

'No?' said the king. 'What do you feel about it — that it's beautiful? Or that it's horrible?'

'Both,' said Daisy. 'But a bit more, that it's beautiful.'

'Then after all,' said Oak, 'you have understood.'

'Does it only work for trees?' Daisy asked.

'Being a tree, I can't say,' said Oak. 'You should know.'

The clearing was now crowded with tree-people. Hawthorn elbowed his way to the middle, and stood beside Oak. 'A crown for a king,' he said, with a sweeping bow that was almost a dance step, and gave Oak a wreath of hawthorn leaves and tiny buds. 'Do you wear it yourself, or do you name another?'

'I wear it myself,' said Oak. 'If I'm chosen.'

The Trees all shouted their choice — it was 'Oak! Oak! Oak!' all round. He put on the hawthorn crown and smiled round at them; they cheered and patted him on the back or shoulder, as many as could reach.

138

'To the queen's tree!' he called above their noise.

'Take your knot,' said Hawthorn busily. He put into each person's hand a little posy of may-buds. The children took theirs in their right hands, as their left still clutched their secret weapons. The whole band, cheerful and singing, set off for the queen's tree; it wasn't a procession, but a jostling, larking crowd.

'I thought the First of May was a religious ceremony,' said Dan to Elder, who was polishing his little reedless pipe on his tunic in an interval in the music.

'So it is,' said Elder, playing a trill of notes.

'It's more like a party,' said Dan. 'Where's the religion?'

'In the songs and dances,' said Elder. 'What do you suppose religion is?'

'More serious,' said Dan. 'Everybody here is laughing.'

'So I should hope,' said Elder. 'The religion is the delight. And the laughter.' He concentrated again on his piping.

Daisy, as the singers pushed their way through close-hanging branches and undergrowth, was engaged in using her eyes, but in growing puzzlement. Finally she edged up close to Blackthorn in the crowd and whispered behind her hand, 'Where are the winter people?'

'They'll meet us later,' said Blackthorn aloud and happily. 'Their time is up!'

'They're plotting a revolution,' said Daisy. 'The queen's got to know.'

'They're always plotting something,' said Blackthorn lightly. 'They can't do anything; it's our time now.' He tossed up, and caught, his posy, and whistled to a chaffinch in a cherry tree. Daisy, looking for the bird, caught sight of Mistletoe behind the tree.

The may-carriers went to the queen's own tree, where Daisy had first seen Ash. Ash's people were standing round, and shouted and sang and clapped a welcome; but there was no sign of Ash herself, and no pile of branches at the foot of the tree.

'She isn't here,' said Daisy, as Hawthorn gave the posies he called knots to all the queen's people.

The Trees near her only laughed.

When each person had their knot, the trees all sang a verse together — a verse the Sturgesses had heard sung once by their school choir:

> We've brought you here a bunch of May
> And at your door we stand:
> It is but a sprout, but it's well budded out,
> By the work of God's own hand.

When the verse was over, complete silence fell; all the tree-people stood gazing with expectation at the queen's tree.

The air in front of the tree began to shimmer — or was the tree vibrating? It was difficult to see. Something, some shape, began to form in the quivering air in front of the tree. It was a mass of ash branches in leaf. The leaves were moving, and among them began to appear a face — shoulders — hands. The leaves dissolved into air, and Ash was standing motionless in front of her tree. Her eyes were closed and she seemed to be asleep. She was very pale and her head drooped a little. She took a couple of uncertain steps forward, like a sleepwalker, and stood still again.

Oak walked up to her. 'In the Rising and the Falling,' he said to her. 'It is time, queen. The balance must be served.' He kissed her, gently and politely, on the forehead, and Ash at once woke — opening her eyes, straightening up, and looking seriously at Oak.

'So the oak is out before the ash,' she said.

'A dry summer,' Oak said, grinning.

'Air and water will see about that,' said Ash, and laughed. Hawthorn crowned her with may, using the same formula as he had done with Oak; and as queen and king stood together the tree-people pelted them with the sprigs of hawthorn from their knots.

140

At the end of this they burst spontaneously into a version of the game 'Nuts in May', which they called 'Knots in May'. The children avoided this, doubting whether they could play one-handed. It was notable that though the two sides started mixed, with men and women in both teams, either by favouring chance or by clever engineering an Ash team, all women, and an Oak team, all men, began to emerge from the struggles.

'They're picking sides for the summer,' said Daisy. 'Only they know which is which to start with.'

'Testing the balance,' suggested Dan. The balance at the end seemed to be good: the game ended with a free-for-all, part tug-of-war and part rugby scrum (with Mistletoe for ball) in which neither side seemed to be victorious.

'And now,' said Ash, pulling out of this and smoothing her tangled hair, 'to the gathering-floor, king. We must hear an account of how the winter people have ruled for us.'

The twins exchanged glances: now perhaps they would have their chance to speak. And act — they were still clutching their weapons.

—— 17 ——

Dan believed he had seen Oak angry before, and Daisy knew she had seen Ash angry. But they became aware of a new dimension of anger when the tree-people, and their may-crowned rulers, got to the gathering-floor.

Oak and Ash were walking ahead, and when they had nearly reached the clearing they came to a jarring halt. There was something about their stillness which quelled the babble of joking and chatting behind them.

Oak spoke, not in a ringing voice but in a sibilant whisper. 'Who has done this?' he said. 'Queen, do you see it?'

'We are barred from our own sacred place!' exploded Ash

— no whispering about her reaction. 'The king and queen through years of summers — we are fenced out.'

'In the heart of the High Forest,' hissed Oak. 'Metal wire! The Death! Who did it? Was it human men?'

Dan and Daisy were suddenly deeply aware that they might be in as great danger from the bright summer people as from the dark winter ones. Had they affronted the balance in some unforgivable way?

'I did it,' said Dan, shouldering his way forward.

'He didn't — I did,' said Daisy, close behind.

'It doesn't mean any harm,' said Dan. 'It was to keep a secret. We —'

'Take it down!' shouted Oak. His voice was a roar. 'Keep your words to yourself. Take the wire down!'

Daisy and Dan rushed to do so. It was a job that needed four hands, and they let go of their weapons; hoping that the influence of the blades would be confused with that of the wire. Dan unwound from one end and Daisy from the other, and when they met Daisy rolled the metal up.

'What will they do to us?' she muttered.

'Nothing, perhaps,' said Dan. 'If it comes to the worst, Daise, we've got fire and air, and I don't think they've got earth and water yet.'

'Then the earth can't open and swallow us up. I hope,' said Daisy.

'There is a hollow ash tree over there,' said the king, who now came into the clearing. 'Put the ball of wire into it, then we can have some peace from it.'

'We're very sorry,' began Dan, while Daisy did this. 'We had good reason for what we did.'

'So you say,' said Oak fiercely. 'You can explain yourselves later. There are things to be done first. Are the winter people here? Sound your drum, Cherry. Let them be called.'

'Oak, we've got to tell you — ' began Dan, touching the king's arm.

Oak shrugged him off. 'Not yet,' he said, with a flash of anger. 'Keep silence. The ritual begins.'

142

Cherry brought out his little drum and played a long roll. There was an answering drumming from away in the woods.

'And you, Maple,' said Ash, and Maple joined in. The answering drumming was nearer this time, and voices were heard singing, drawing close. First, ahead of the drumming, a robin came flying a zigzag course into the clearing; and after it the winter people came dancing in. They exchanged handshakes and jokes with the summer people, and there was a lot of laughter and good-natured foolery. As there might be between any two armies meeting sociably during a truce. The children kept well in the background, and watched especially to see how Oak and Holly would meet: murdered and murderer, Daisy still felt. They exchanged a quick, rough hug like two successful footballers, and Oak — the taller of the two — gave Holly a little friendly shake. 'Well, now, to business,' he said. Ash and Ivy, sharing a hug of their own, drew apart at once. The four main actors stood in a little group; the other Trees, winter and summer mingled together, made a wide circle around them and the fire-stone, and stopped their greetings to listen.

Ivy and Holly bowed to the other two. 'We have ruled in peace, Summer King and Queen,' said Holly. 'There were no disturbances.'

'Fifteen dead and one living fell in a gale,' said Ivy. 'The oldest lime of all has lost a limb. Spring has come late, but the sleepers are out of their sleep — hedgehogs and squirrels and mouse folk.'

'We lit the new year's light; and held the Turning, and the festivals,' said Holly. 'As well as the fire-festival could be held, lacking the fire-cross.'

'They didn't,' said a voice among the Trees. 'They failed to hold the festival of air. There was no wind-riding, and no scattering of the ashes of the year's dead.' Hazel pushed through the other Trees and stood defiantly confronting Ivy.

'You weren't asked,' said Ivy coldly. 'What do you know about it?'

143

'Asked or not, I was there,' said Hazel. 'You neglected the festival of air.'

'True — they did,' Bramble's voice called from the throng.

'We had a difficulty, dear lady,' said Holly earnestly to Ash. 'We couldn't hold the festival properly: by then we were fenced out of here by the human witnesses. We did what we could.'

'Let it pass,' said Ash. 'Is that all?'

'We have no more to say,' said Ivy. 'We kept good rule for you.'

'And now, Holly,' said Oak, 'kneel to me as you ought and render up my dominion.'

Holly stood stiffly, a little way away from Oak, and didn't take the pebble pendant from his neck. Oak took the axe from Mistletoe, weighed it in his hand and gave it back.

'No need of strokes from me to you, Holly,' he said with an easy grin. 'My time has come, and you know me for your lord. In the Rising and the Falling, render me my dominion, and go free and peaceful into the summer.'

'No,' said Holly. He stared at Oak unblinking, sharp teeth showing between red lips.

Oak stared at him, motionless but apparently totally disconcerted. Years of well-observed ritual had not prepared him for this.

'You serve the balance,' he said to Holly.

'I challenge the balance,' said Holly. 'My people increase, and yours diminish. I grow in numbers and in kinds.'

'As I do,' said Ivy to Ash. 'I stand with him: we challenge your rule.' Her long fingers twitched by her sides.

'Then let's fight,' said Ash, eagerly. 'Give us our dominions, Holly and Ivy; arm yourselves; and we'll meet in battle. Bow to bow.'

'No bows,' said Ivy shortly. 'We fight with the dominions.'

'You mean you would use the dominions as weapons?' asked Oak, incredulous. 'We should die in thousands, trees of all species. Yours as well as mine: you couldn't discriminate. You would outrage the balance.'

'I repeat,' said Holly, 'I challenge the balance. I have fire and earth — oh yes, Oak, the fire-cross is found. Ivy has water and air. Give up your right to them, and let them be Ivy's and mine for ever — ours and our people's. Or suffer. You are defenceless, except for your feeble bows and spears. Fight, and you will be massacred.'

Oak stood steady. 'I don't believe you would do it, even though you threaten,' he said. 'Fight with the dominions! It's a blasphemy.'

For answer, Holly held the pendant between both his hands and stamped on the ground. The earth shook under their feet; and with a rumbling crash the shell of the hollow ash where Daisy had put the wire came down, and its hulk broke and flattened some saplings under it.

'Enough,' said Oak impassively. His eyes glittered and the set of his jaw was grim, but his anger was an inward anger now. 'You challenge the balance: let the balance answer you. Do you give Ash and me any chance to confer?'

'As much as you like — up to an hour,' said Holly. 'But no chance to leave this place and go to your halls for weapons — you or the children. We shall surround you.'

'As you like,' said Oak. 'Leave us private.'

The winter people drew away to the outskirts of the clearing, and the summer people gathered near the fire-stone, round Oak and Ash.

'It looks bad, my dear people,' said Oak. 'If they use earth against us, landslips may tear us out of the hillsides; if they use water, floods may wash us up by the roots; if they use air, whirlwinds may uproot us. Any kind of uprooting is death. And if they use fire, we shall die as blackened stumps. Fire and air together are deadliest of all.'

'It has been forbidden from all time to use the dominions in war,' said Ash. 'A curse will fall on them, if they do this.'

'Of course,' said Oak. 'The balance will avenge us, over the years. But you, queen, and I, and our proud, brave people,

145

will die like that fallen ancient.' He nodded to the old ash trunk.

'You don't have to,' said Daisy. She dodged herself clear of Trees, and towed Dan with her up to Ash and Oak. 'You needn't be massacred!'

'It looks all too likely, for all your hopeful words,' said Oak. 'You were meant to be our witnesses, you and Aidan. You may be witness of our deaths, and die with us in the witnessing.'

'No, we won't,' said Daisy. 'Tell him, Dan!'

Dan fetched out of his pocket a much-swaddled bundle, unrolled several dingy handkerchiefs and offered the pieces of the fire-cross to Oak in his cupped hands.

'O king,' he began. It was undoubtedly correct but it sounded silly. He cleared his throat and began again.

'It's the right one: I've tried it,' he said. 'It wasn't lost. They had it, under the stone.'

'Drop it into my hands,' said Oak softly. 'Don't let any watchers see. Stocks and stones! We have a fighting chance!'

'You've got more than that,' said Daisy. 'You've got the deadliest of all. This is yours, Ash.' And she laid her right hand over the queen's and drew it away leaving Ash holding the sky-blue, glistening air.

In spite of herself, Ash gave a shout of joy. 'Queen among warriors!' she said with delight to Daisy, who at once self-consciously bunched back her trailing hair with her spare hand. 'Oak, Oak, the balance is restored!'

'We care about the balance too,' said Daisy shyly. 'Though we don't understand it.'

'Do first, understand afterwards,' said Ash. 'That's the great rule of religion. Otherwise you wouldn't start. You who were meant to be witnesses have acted best of all, and become our saviours. Did you steal it?'

'At the Turning feast,' said Daisy. 'I thought they'd killed you, and I took it away to spite them.'

'And then we went to look for the lost thing,' said Dan.

146

'What we guessed was, Mistletoe took it and Holly and Ivy had hidden it. They caught us and they wanted us to fight for them — with the Death.'

'But we wouldn't,' added Daisy. 'We tried to tell you, earlier.'

'So you did,' said the king. 'I understand you now. Fight with the Death! Fight with the dominions! They are traitors to the trees' good, and not fit to be called wooden. Cherry, sound your drum: we'll call them back.'

Cherry drummed, and Holly and Ivy came back into the centre of the gathering-floor. Their people, the children noticed, remained as guards, posted at intervals around the clearing's edge. They had fetched weapons from a cache: each Tree held bow or spear.

'Well?' said Holly to Oak, with a nervous insolence. 'Do you give in?'

'Do you hold by what you said? That you would use all four dominions against us, and massacre us unarmed?' asked Oak.

'Indeed he does,' said Ivy. 'If you are massacred, it will be your own fault. You have only to surrender your claim to the four dominions to us for ever, and we will let you go in safety.'

'A pretty logic,' said Ash, 'to call us guilty of our own death if we don't give in and so are massacred! Your acts are your acts, Ivy, whether or not they are provoked — which this is not. Our death is on your head for ever, if we die.'

'Do you defy us, then?' said Holly to Oak.

'We do defy you,' said Oak.

'Then you stand to be massacred, every living tree. Root and branch, heartwood and sapwood. And the meddling children,' said Holly.

'As you like,' said Oak indifferently. 'Remind me first, Holly: which combination of powers would you call most sinister? Earth and air, would it be? Water and fire?'

'You're only playing for time, asking us riddling questions,'

147

said Ivy. 'I'll answer what every Tree of us knows. Air and fire are worst: the fire the wind drives is irresistible.'

'Watch,' said Oak. He and Ash both raised their right hands, each holding something. A great blaze of fire, like a burning ball, leapt from Oak's hands into the air; it hung for a moment and then flew, spinning, into the branches of a young holly tree. There was a soft, explosive roar and the whole tree burst into flames.

'Rain, Ivy, rain!' cried Holly.

'No rain,' said Ash. 'I've blown the sky clear.'

Two things happened almost at once. Ivy leapt to the fire-stone and single-handed raised one end of it, peering underneath. 'It's gone — the cross!' she called to Holly. 'He's got it.' Holly, enraged, sprang towards Oak, but recollected himself and stood still, close to Oak, confronting him.

'So you have fire,' he said. 'But I still have earth. And you will die through it. The earth will open at your feet, you arrogant trunk, and your tree will fall and rot. I have only to stamp my foot.'

'Stamp it,' said Oak coolly. 'My death won't matter.'

'You've had one warning,' said Ivy, running to stand beside Holly. 'A demonstration, now. No more words, Holly: action!'

Both of them raised their clasped hands above their heads and shouted — with a wordless, high-pitched yell which sounded like the most primitive of all battle-cries. Their eyes were fixed on their hands. All the other Trees stared at them, but braced themselves (some intertwining stiff arms with their neighbours) as if they knew what was to come.

This time the earth did not merely shake. There came from under the gathering-floor a sound as of rocks grinding and clashing together, as of splitting and falling. In the very centre of the clearing, where the fire-stone stood, the ground heaved and burst open into a huge crevasse, and into this the fire-stone disappeared together with much of the earth around it. From the dark crevasse water sprang up like a geyser and showered the Trees with ice-cold rivulets.

Holly was laughing with pleasure and singing, between his teeth, 'The Holly and the Ivy'. Dan, steadying himself against Daisy as the ground still shivered, turned towards Oak and saw horror mixed with the fury in the king's face.

He never, afterwards, entirely understood his own motives. But at the time there seemed only one thing to do. He freed his penknife and leapt at Holly, stabbing at the upraised hands which still held the pebble pendant of earth. The laugh in Holly's mouth turned to an oath and he shied away abruptly, letting the pebble go; and in that moment, lightning-quick, Dan cut its leather thong, caught it and threw it to Oak, who caught it dexterously.

'Now me,' said Daisy, and ran towards Ivy. She shut her mind to the mask of malice on Ivy's features and aimed, as Dan had done, for the clutching hands. But Ivy, tricky as ever, had seen what she would do. As Daisy raced towards her a ground-runner of ivy caught Daisy's ankle like a snare; Daisy fell headlong and her scissors went into Ivy's foot. Ivy shrieked and her hands went down to the injured foot, dropping the ring which had been folded between them. As Daisy reached for it, Ivy kicked it away.

'Take it, if you can get it,' she said. 'Water on its own is a feeble weapon, and I know it. It's worth nothing.'

Ash sprang forward then, to take back her own. But as she was off her guard and stooping, Ivy recovered herself and leapt at her. One arm hooked around Ash's neck; one hand struck at Ash's hand which held air. Ash hung on to air, clasping it in a clenched fist, and fought to shake Ivy off her back. Other Trees shouted and closed round; and in the hurly-burly Dan saw, out of the corner of his eye, Mistletoe sliding towards the Oak King. He held behind his back the stone-headed axe, and as Dan took in his movements he realized that Mistletoe was swinging it up preparatory to hurling it at the back of Oak's head. Before his arm came right up, Dan flung himself on his back; his right hand grabbed

Mistletoe's arm, his left reached for his left shoulder. Dan's left hand was still full of penknife and Mistletoe was scratched — a very minor scratch — somewhere around his left shoulder-blade. Mistletoe screamed and the axe flew wide; it caught Ivy in the right arm and she slid away from Ash and fell heavily to the ground.

As if nothing had interrupted her, Ash gathered up her ring and put it on.

'It's worth something to me,' she said. 'Sweet springs, and running rivers; my own black pool, my lovely waterfall.' She spread her fingers and looked at the ring with satisfaction; Oak watched her, pleased.

Taking stock, the children saw that the winter people were all hemmed in — each of them sandwiched between two summer Trees, and their weapons gone. The summer people had acted quickly when they saw their chance. Mistletoe and Ivy had both picked themselves up, Ivy apparently collected and calm, Mistletoe shaking with shock and frustration.

'Yes — Mistletoe,' said Oak, fondling the pendant which now hung round his neck. 'Come out where I can see you, Mistletoe; stand with him, Holly and Ivy. We have a few things to discuss. Sheathe up your weapons, witnesses. You have begun to redress the centuries' wrongdoing of your race.'

'What will you do with us?' said Holly, resting an arm on Ivy's shoulders. 'Our lives are forfeit.'

'Your lives are always forfeit, in the spring,' said Oak. 'I've never needed to show my power by striking you dead yet, Holly, and I shan't do so now. The balance judges you. If you are strong enough to defy the balance, you are too strong, and must be weakened. Your followers must be reduced: you must include only the true foresters, and shut the extra people out.'

'You and Ivy both,' said Ash. 'We shall watch you: we shall know what you do.'

'As for any further judgement on you, let it wait. The

150

queen and I will consult our Councils,' said Oak grandly.

Ivy nodded, silent, and Holly shrugged. There was something about them both which suggested immense relief: they had expected death or banishment.

'And you, Mistletoe,' said Oak. 'I dislike what I discover about you. You have been among my people, acting as my man; but now I learn that you are allied with the winter people.'

'I'm nobody's man, but everybody's friend,' said Mistletoe ingratiatingly. 'Welcome everywhere, universally useful. That's me.'

'No, it isn't,' said Ivy clearly — and many of the summer Trees murmured their agreement. 'He's a spy and a nuisance. A failed assassin. Not one of us; he was never one of us.'

'You must decide,' insisted Oak. 'Summer or winter?'

'How can I decide?' said Mistletoe truly distressed. 'I grow on oak and apple, summer trees. I'm greeny-gold all winter. I have to be both.'

'Then I'll decide for you,' said Oak. 'You hold with the winter Trees, Mistletoe; your actions prove it. You stole fire; you plotted our downfall; you raised the axe to me. You are cut off from Ash's court and mine.'

Mistletoe wept, large pearly tears. They seemed quite genuine.

'Moreover,' said Oak, 'you had better take a full Tree's part. Forget your rootlessness, the fact that you are different; you've hidden behind that long enough. I shall give you a job to do and a responsibility to carry.'

Dan jogged Oak's elbow. 'Don't, don't!' he whispered. 'He's not fit to be trusted.'

'Of course not,' Oak whispered back. 'Because nobody's ever trusted him. I shall give him a trust. It will balance him.'

Baffled, Dan moved away, irrelevantly wondering what had been in Mr Briggs's head when he made Jenk form captain.

'You will watch the balance, Mistletoe, in the winter court,'

151

said Oak. 'You are one of the winter people — but it will be your charge to serve the balance first.'

Mistletoe rubbed his face dry. 'Can I still guard the axe?' he asked childishly.

'Why not?' said Oak briefly. 'Pick it up. Join your people. And let all the winter ones go to their own place; we of the summer have our things to celebrate.'

'They're back on form,' Daisy whispered to Dan. 'They're going to have a party.'

Summer

— 18 —

The first of May was the second and last time, in the whole of the year's adventure, that Mr and Mrs Sturgess organized a search-party to look for the twins. When the children weren't home by eight o'clock, and Mrs Sturgess was already washing up the breakfast things, mild panic descended and the family set up an instant twin-hunt. So it was that Daisy and Dan, rambling home wearing hawthorn crowns conferred on them by Oak, carrying their duffel-coats, arm in arm and singing the round 'Come follow', were met by a rather annoyed father and a slightly annoyed sister.

'We're quite all right, Dad,' said Daisy hastily. 'Did you think we'd died and the robins had covered us up with leaves? We just lost count of time a bit. We had all sorts of special May games.'

'What, all this time?' said Margaret, and Mr Sturgess said, 'Where's everybody else?'

At this the twins laughed helplessly: since the truth was that they were part of an elbowing, singing throng who were at that moment bellowing, 'To the greenwood — to the greenwood — to the greenwood, greenwood tree!' at the tops of their Tree voices.

'You won't get any sense out of them, Dad,' said Margaret. 'I used to get like that when I was thirteen.'

Mrs Sturgess nearly bundled them out of the house again when she saw them wearing may.

'Don't bring that in here!' she exclaimed. 'Don't you know it's unlucky to bring hawthorn into the house? It's supposed to be the fairies' flower.'

'Oh, it's all right for us, Mum,' said Dan, and Daisy had to cover this with, 'He means, it's all right today. It's not unlucky on the first of May.'

155

'Take it off, anyway,' said Margaret. 'You look like the Green Man in the church. I'm not going indoors with heathen deities.'

'We've got to go in', grumbled Dan. 'Our school clobber's inside.'

Margaret, as usual, went off without them, and the two were briefly alone on their way to the bus.

'We've only got May and June — until the evening of Midsummer Day — with the Trees,' said Daisy to Dan as they hurried along. 'I shall hate it when our year-and-a-day's over. Think of being in the Forest and having no idea whether the Trees were about or not. What a frost.'

'Today was glorious,' Dan agreed. 'But I don't see how Oak is ever going to keep the peace with the winter people now. Do you?'

'It sounds a bit iffy,' said Daisy. 'But what can we do?'

'I don't know. Something. I mean to talk to Oak,' said Dan.

True to his word, Dan went out into the Forest when he next had free time, in search of Oak. He found many of the summer people, but most of them were in a strange, abstracted state where he could get little sense out of them. They wandered about little better than sleep-walkers, eyes unfocused, and concentration was not to be had from them. Oak was the most promising, when Dan finally persuaded Bramble to take him where Oak was. The king was sitting under his own tree, alone, his elbows on his knees and his chin on his hands, and staring into the deeps of the Forest through a gap between trees.

'Can I talk to you, Oak?' said Dan hopefully.

Oak seemed not to hear, so Dan patted his shoulder gently.

Oak wasn't pleased at being disturbed. 'What is it?' he said. 'Don't come and bother me now. Or any of us. It's the time of messages.'

'What messages?' asked Dan.

'Come at the middle of June,' said Oak. 'Not in May. How can I hear what you say, when the air's full of messages?'

156

'What does he mean? I can't follow him,' Dan complained to Bramble. His feelings were somewhat bruised by his being ignored.

'It's the main flowering time,' said Bramble, who seemed more collected than most of them. 'The air is full of pollen, and deafening to us with humming insects, and thick with the scents of all the blossoms. Tree-people go about drunk with it. Except, of course, for those whose flowering is earlier — like Hazel; he wakes up for his in January, poor fellow, and some of the queen's people are in bloom very early, too. But for most of us it's now. I think you'd call it being in love.'

'Oh,' said Dan. 'But Blackthorn said individuals don't love and want to get married, among the Trees.'

'Well, no,' Bramble, said. 'It's a collective thing. It's all in the air; the air's all messages now. But the individual Trees are dazed and dizzy with it, all the same. Don't you notice it yourself?'

Dan observed. The Forest was full of shafts of sunlight, and streams of warm, delicious air; but to him it smelled mainly clean and leafy. Bluebells and wild orchis caught his eye most. It was also full of birdsong and tiny insects; and motes of dust or pollen showed in the streaks of light.

'A bit, I think,' he said cautiously. 'But I'd notice it more if it was, say, a field of beans.'

'A field of beans!' said Bramble, amazed. 'The power of that is colossal. I can hardly stand up on my feet if I smell *that*. It's just to avoid things like that that I keep to the middle Forest.'

Dan went home disappointed. 'They're all in love,' he said to Daisy. 'Only they call it the messages. It's useless. I'm to try again in June.'

'So there's nothing doing all May?' asked Daisy.

'That's about it,' said Dan. 'It's just as well, I suppose, as we've got exams this term.'

By the middle of June, with exams over and summer projects not begun, there was a short lull in school life. Daisy was

157

involved with Patsy and Monica in the intricacies of the royal wedding in Hugoland; Terry's bike was in for repairs and Dan was bored. He made one or two sallies into the Forest on fine evenings after school, but hardly anybody seemed to be about. On one of these he saw Yew, not far from Fosters; Yew waved and came towards him. Not certain how he would be received, Dan pretended he hadn't seen and ducked in to the church, with a recollection that people were safe from pursuit in churches.

'Sanctuary,' he said to himself; and he went and stood by the last column on the left and looked up at the foliate head.

'Well? Do you like him?' said a voice at his side. Oak was there, having come silent out of the shadows of the south aisle.

'Him? Or you?' said Dan. 'He looks a bit fierce, I think. Forbidding. He might sentence you to death.'

'And carry out the sentence,' said Oak. 'I might. If I needed to.'

'I didn't know you came in here,' said Dan. 'If somebody came in now, I'd be talking to myself; they'd think I was off my head.'

'Those who've been a while in the Forest are often supposed to be mad,' said Oak. 'I don't come in here often. Because of Them.' He nodded towards the tower.

'Them? Who?' Dan asked.

'That weight of metal — the menace of it!' said Oak. 'They are giants. I can feel their strength even outside the door; and when they peal, all of us Trees go up into the High Forest to be well away.'

'Oh — the bells!' said Dan. 'Why did you come in, then?'

'To see that,' said the king. He led Dan up to the memorial window with its red-and-gold tree. 'Tell me what the writing says.'

Dan was taken aback. But after all, who would teach a Tree to read? Why should he or she need to?

Oak was pleased when Dan read him the inscription. 'It's about the balance,' he said. 'Why is it there?'

158

'In memory of warriors,' said Dan, 'who died in wars.'

'Fighting for the balance?' said the king keenly. Dan wasn't too sure, but he thought he had better agree. 'In a way,' he said.

'Of course,' said Oak. 'And why were you hunting for me? Sit down on this wood and tell me your thoughts.'

They sat side-by-side in a pew. There was something pleasantly ridiculous about Oak's majestic bulk on the narrow, shelf-like seat with its strip of carpet.

'It's about the winter people,' said Dan. 'I'm worried. What's to stop them trying again, next winter? And if they try when they really have all four dominions, won't they win hands down?'

'I am in a new world,' said the king. 'When the balance is served, the balance will assert itself sooner or later. Years, and trees, rise and fall; the balance itself does not change. But in a world where the dominions could be used in battle, and Trees make war with the Death, I no longer know what is possible and what is not. The queen and I, who have lived by our traditions, now have to live by our wits.'

'And our wits,' said Dan. 'Mine and Diana's.'

'Naturally,' said the king. 'You serve the balance. Not as tools, but because you see what is good.'

'Or who,' said Dan.

Oak laughed, but briefly. 'What we have to fear is that the Trees' part in the balance will alter,' he said.

'Could that happen?' Dan asked.

'Oh yes,' said Oak. 'Part of what the winter people said was true. Their numbers continually increase, ours dwindle. Your people make it so. If they come to outnumber us absurdly, the Forest balance may finally alter. Moreover, by what human beings do, the numbers of trees of all kinds go down from year to year — from day to day, even. We are felled for trade; we are felled to make space for crops, houses, roads for wheels — anything. If trees grow too few to rule, who will rule after us? Who has our wisdom about times and seasons, and our knowledge of festivals? If the winter Trees

159

rule perpetually, there may be perpetual winter. If nobody rules, there may be chaos — a spring without green leaves, an autumn without fruit. No crops for you, no leafy dew for us. Custom would go and the last of the common culture die. Even your human festivals.'

'No Christmas!' said Dan.

'A Christmas without songs or candles, anyhow,' Oak answered.

'So what can you do?' said Dan. 'They've proved they have too much power — I understand that. Can you really limit it?'

'You'll see,' said Oak. 'Within the balance, the queen and I can act: we are still their masters.'

'Is there any chance at all that they could be your friends?' Dan asked. 'Were they, ever?'

'Never,' said the king. 'Enmity between summer and winter is in the balance itself; one pulls against the other as dark pulls against light.'

'Even so,' said Dan, 'you and Ash are enemies sometimes, but somehow stay friends. Couldn't you and the winter Trees be the same?'

'Never, never,' said Oak, his whole face stiffening into a frown. 'Summer and winter serve different ends.'

Dan sighed. 'But if you never see them, you can't keep an eye on what they're doing,' he said. 'Why aren't they part of things when you're in command? Like your festivals. They didn't come to water or earth — why not? And we didn't see them about all last summer.'

'They were around,' said Oak. 'But they kept well clear of our war. They have their own festivals; it's traditional that they don't come to ours.'

'If they were involved a bit more, you could be sure they were keeping the truce,' said Dan. 'They're awake, aren't they? Not like you in the winter.'

'Mostly awake,' said Oak. 'They rest at intervals. They are avoiding us summer people, now. Part of our judgement on them — mine and the queen's — has still to be pronounced.'

160

'Are you going to execute anyone?' asked Dan, thinking of the stone axe.

'Not this year,' said Oak. 'If for some years their power is decreased, we shall see if they learn a little balance for themselves. We know how we shall attempt it; you'll enjoy the logic of it, I feel sure. And we shall take one of their followers for ourselves. You can advise me. Which one shall it be?'

'Some of them don't seem very nice,' said Dan. 'They treat Larch and Fir rather as slaves, because they aren't Old Ones. Holly talks like a patronizing uncle but he and Ivy are actually quite ferocious. I'd have Larch, I think. She doesn't seem to hate you, and at least she has a sense of humour.'

'And moreover, she's mainly deciduous,' said Oak. 'The queen is of your opinion. She would welcome Larch.'

'When are you going to do your final judgement?' Dan asked.

'There must be an extra festival,' said Oak. 'The winter dances were not properly completed, and air was never held at all. We must send for them some time for the wind-riding; the judgement could be then.'

'Make it soon,' said Dan. 'Invite them for Midsummer. Treat them like friends, even if they aren't. You've got to live with them somehow till next November — and every summer afterwards. There'd be more chance of peace if you didn't live as strangers. I served the balance in May: maybe I'm serving it now. You ought to listen.'

'You speak as an animal,' said Oak. 'But I have listened. I shall talk to the queen.'

Dan had to be satisfied with that. He set off for home; and this time, mindful of his own theories, he looked for Yew and called out when he saw him. Yew came up eagerly. Who should apologize to whom? In the end neither of them said anything: they shook hands awkwardly and each went on his way.

Daisy was waiting for Dan in the lane outside Fosters when he got back.

161

'I've thought what to do,' she said abruptly. 'Aidan, we must have a party.'

'What, us?' said Dan. 'We're the ones who go to parties.'

'That's what I mean,' said Daisy. 'We went to June, and November, and December, and May. Now our year-and-a-day's almost up, we ought to have the Trees to a party of our own.'

'How can we manage it?' grumbled Dan. 'No — wait, though, Diana. We ought, you're right, and we'll have the winter people too.'

'Won't they be huffy? Or actually fight?' Daisy asked.

From what Oak said, I don't think they'll actually fight,' Dan answered. 'They've got to get over being huffy some time; and the sooner the better.'

'As for how we'll manage it, I don't know,' said Daisy.

It was easy. As the family sat over supper, Mrs Sturgess said to the younger ones, 'Your Dad and I are thinking of going to Douglas again for our wedding anniversary — staying a night as we did last year, and having an evening out.'

'Oh, Mum, you can't!' said Margaret, dismayed. 'At least — of course you can, but I'm going to the Melbury Midsummer Ball with Jamie and it goes on until all hours — two or three in the morning. I forgot it would be your anniversary, and I meant to stay with Jamie's mother afterwards. So what about the twins?'

'We'll be all right,' said Dan at once. 'We're teenagers now, don't forget. We don't need a baby-sitter.'

'You're not staying here alone half the night, all the same,' said their father. 'This house is too isolated — it's not as if you had good neighbours close at hand.'

'Well — what about neighbours?' said Daisy. 'Aidan and I can go to the Markhams.' (Dan looked gloomy.) 'They've just got a little caravan, and it's in the paddock. I'm sure they'd let us stay there a night, and it's right by their house. We could take sleeping-bags.'

'A caravan!' said Dan, perking up at once. He had never slept in a caravan.

162

'And if it's a nice evening,' Daisy went on relentlessly, 'can we have a party in the garden here? Just a small one?'

'A disco?' said Mr Sturgess. 'They'd hear *that* at Markhams', and beyond.'

'*Not* a disco,' said Dan, thinking of all that metal. 'Country dancing and silly games.'

'Good grief,' said his father. 'What are teenagers coming to?'

—— 19 ——

It was a superb party.

It was, in fact, Dan's and Daisy's second party of the evening. They realized that in order to have one party, they had to have two: one visible one, for friends in the village; and one invisible one, for the Trees. As preparations for the Tree-party had to be made, the whisper of a Sturgess party would go round the village, and Markham and Jenkins and other feelings be hurt if invitations didn't arrive.

The first party started at six and ate crisps, sausage rolls and cheese straws, and drank mild cider and coke; it used the kitchen and the garden. It had music provided by a record-player but its most successful feature was 'Murder' played in the shrubby and shadowy part of the garden. As promised to all parents, it was over by ten; and as promised to Sturgess parents, the twins were in bed in the caravan by ten thirty. The Markhams had kindly provided them with a small blue night-light, in case they should wake and wonder where they were; by its glow, with a good deal of giggling, the twins got up again at half-past eleven and in track suits and trainers crept across the humpy (and in places thistly) paddock and got into the lane for home.

Food and drink for the second party had been a problem.

'We can't give them what they usually have,' said Dan. 'If

we tried to provide earth, we'd get it all wrong; and leafy dew must take days to collect.'

'No, it's got to be something different,' said Daisy. 'But all vegetable. They could never drink coke: think, coming out of those tins it would taste of metal to them. For all we know, it's made of metal. It tastes like it.'

'Orange squash?' suggested Dan. 'No, that won't do: our water comes out of taps.'

'Real orange and apple juice,' said Daisy. 'The milkman brings it in cartons. It says 'pure' on it, so it ought to be all right.'

'And fruit,' said Dan. 'I wonder if they'd eat biscuits?'

'If we made them ourselves,' said Daisy. 'Flour's all right, and sugar; they come from plants. We could use a sunflower-oil fat instead of butter, and no milk.'

'Tree biscuits,' said Dan. 'I wonder what they'll be like?'

'We can put spice in,' said Daisy. 'Just so long as the tree-people don't taste oven when they eat them.'

'Maybe it'd wear off if they were carefully cooled,' said Dan. 'Not on wire trays. What about glasses?'

'It might be safest to have paper cups,' said Daisy. 'Plates are all right. Crockery's made out of clay.'

'Then there's our secret peace kit,' said Dan. He and Daisy whispered and laughed. 'The ultimate deterrent,' said Daisy. 'But we mustn't get anything that comes in a tin.'

Both children felt that invitations had to be personally issued. They both hunted the Forest until they found summer and winter people, hes and shes, and asked for the message to be spread around.

'Message!' said Ash to Daisy, amused. 'We're almost out of the time of messages. And it's long since we last visited with witnesses. We shall be glad to come. We'll come to you at midnight, as you suggest, and put off our Turning, and our wind-riding and water-dancing, until just before dawn.'

Prompt at midnight, the Trees arrived. The children, carrying out the last of the food, heard soft voices; and then louder joking as the visitors leapt the garden gate — no passing between metal catch and hinges for them. They were in their usual festival high spirits, and the party was a non-stop success. Fruit juice, fruit and nuts-and-raisins were immediately enjoyed; biscuits were eaten with a little doubt at first, but growing appreciation. The twins taught the Trees 'Strip the Willow' and 'Will you go Walk the Woods so Wild' (another dance, chosen for its name — but it had a most catchy tune, and the children didn't need to sing it for long: Silver Birch and Elder soon picked it up and played it.) They also taught some new games: 'Tiggy Touchwood', which seemed appropriate, and a tree-based version of 'Feet off Ground'.

'And now,' said Daisy, as everyone leaned, sat or sprawled in a pause, 'Aidan and I are going to make a speech. It's to thank you for making us warriors and witnesses. We didn't expect to like it, but in the end we did.'

'Most of it, anyway,' Dan added honestly. 'And after tomorrow, when we don't see you there, the Forest will seem empty and strange. Thanks for having us.'

'Warriors are for a season,' said Ash from where she sat, her back against the trunk of a flowering cherry. 'Witnesses are for ever. You'll find you won't be able to forget us.'

'We never will,' said Daisy. 'Even when the Forest seems quiet, we'll know you're there.'

'Witnesses were on both sides,' said Oak, who rested on one elbow near the queen. 'It was an exchange. We learned from you things we didn't know about human life — or had forgotten. We are very cool people, as you know. But we learned that brother and sister is good — like having a friend in a battle.'

The children felt slightly guilty. Dan thought of how Daisy had never been offered a ride on Terry's bike; Daisy, how Dan had never been invited into Hugoland. But the year of the Trees had, it was true, been more brotherly-sisterly — even though they had been on different sides in the war of the Trees.

165

'The queen and I have speeches to make as well,' said Oak, sitting upright. 'First, we must clear the air by settling all questions of judgement.'

'We're all here,' said Ash. 'Now is the moment to declare to the winter Trees what their future is to be.'

'Oh dear,' Daisy whispered to Dan. 'This'll spoil the party.'

'You never know,' Dan whispered back. 'And it had got to happen some time.'

All the Trees were now sitting up straight and looking anxious — even the summer ones.

'First, the question of power,' said Ash. 'For all the long years the Trees remember, Holly and Ivy have held rule in the winter when the summer people rest. They must still do so: the balance demands it. But not in such a way that the balance can be overset, because such an outcome is absurd.'

'So our judgement is,' said Oak (Holly and Ivy exchanged quick, apprehensive glances) 'that at the autumn Change only earth and water shall be given into the hands of the winter Trees. Fire and air are to have other guardians.'

'But who — who?' Ivy burst out, white and dismayed. 'With whom will they ever be safe, if not the winter Trees?'

'With those who won them by their wits,' said Oak, now smiling. 'From November to May, Diana guards air and Aidan, fire. They won them; they can hold them. And the balance will be maintained.'

The whole assembly, including the children, appeared to be thunderstruck; Oak and Ash enjoyed their dramatic coup, and grinned at each other.

'Us!' said Dan, recovering his speech and some measure of intelligence. 'We'll do our best. We'll do it properly. What about when we're grown-up, though?'

'One year at a time,' said Ash.

'So we have another year and a day, do we? We go on being part of the real, secret Forest?' Daisy asked.

'Certainly,' said Ash. 'You have served it well.'

166

'Three cheers!' said Daisy. 'I hate goodbyes. I thought this was a farewell party, and now it isn't.'

'It's a responsibility,' Dan said to her seriously.

'Well, of course,' said Daisy. 'But it's thrilling.'

'And it means we get a chance to patch up a better relationship between us and Holly and Ivy,' Dan added.

'If it's possible,' Daisy said.

'We'll find out,' said Dan.

The summer Trees crowded around the children to pat and congratulate them, but Oak called them off.

The winter Trees were sitting silent and glum, and Ash now spoke to them again.

'One other thing,' she said. 'The king and I have decided that we shall take one Tree of yours into our own courts. Not simply as a hostage, but as a witness; to understand us and our ways. All summer long your Tree will live with us, and return to you in winter to be our interpreter to you.'

Mistletoe got importantly to his feet, puffing out his chest.

'It's me you mean, isn't it?' he said. 'I'm a winter Tree now. I'll come and interpret you.'

'Not you, Mistletoe; sit down,' said Ash sharply. 'You are two-faced enough already; and after your recent treacheries you would not be welcome to us. We have chosen Larch to come if Larch is willing.'

Larch jumped to her feet. 'I'll come,' she said, and then looked back in confusion at Holly and Ivy. Ivy nodded to her, and said tersely, 'Go where you're called. The vanquished have no choice.'

Larch went up to Ash and Oak and bowed her acceptance to them; they both hugged her with massive, crushing hugs. Larch's head came half-way up Oak's huge chest and Dan found himself feeling glad Oak had never hugged him like that — wouldn't he have ended with cracked ribs or a dislocated jaw? Larch seemed to enjoy it, or at least to tolerate it well.

'You have not spoken,' said Oak to Holly and Ivy. 'You have a right to speak.'

167

Holly got up, and dusted his knees in an unconcerned manner. 'Nothing remains to be said,' he replied. 'As Ivy says, we get no choice.'

Ivy sprang up too, pushing Holly aside and interrupting him. 'You've never given our true place to Holly and me,' she said; 'you've always tried to smother us and put us down. Now you turn even our winter powers into a mockery: we're not to be even your equals in show! You set hatred between us.'

'My colleague goes a little too far,' said Holly. 'We don't of course want to indulge in hatred.'

Ivy looked as though she'd like to say, 'Oh yes we do,' but forced herself to keep quiet.

'There's not hatred on our side, and we hope there will be no need for further hostility — beyond what is in our natures, and part of the trees' good,' said Ash. 'We want truce, and all our people with us.'

'And so do we,' said Daisy. 'Where is it, Dan?'

Dan drew a hand out of his pocket. 'This,' he said with a look of triumph, 'is the pipe of peace. It's a vow of long-term truce — a vow taken on fire.'

'Taken on fire!' exclaimed the Trees.

It was a long-discarded pipe of Mr Sturgess's, filled with tobacco obtained by disembowelling a few cigarettes accidentally left behind by Douglas at Christmas. Dan lit it and set it circulating. The Trees were deeply suspicious of the smoke and seemed to dislike both taste and smell (so did the children come to that) but they dutifully puffed and hid their grimaces. As the pipe passed from Oak to Ivy to Ash to Holly to Bramble to Mistletoe and so on, Dan whispered to Daisy, 'It must be all right, mustn't it? Red Indians do it; they live in huge forests, they must know about trees.'

'Did,' said Daisy. 'Lots of them live in towns and villages now. I've seen them in the *National Geographic*. But as all the Trees think the pipe is very nasty, I expect it will work; like brown cough mixture.'

168

'Anyhow,' said Dan, 'if we and the Trees all believe it will work, it *will* work. Peace from now on.'

'All that lovely fighting!' said Daisy with a sigh of regret.

'Getting shot. Beastly earthquakes,' Dan reminded her.

'Oh well,' said Daisy.

After the pipe was out and the suppressed laughter and coughing were over, Oak and Ash rose and all the tree-people got up after them.

'We must leave now,' said Ash. 'For the wind-riding and the water-dancing, and the lighting of the fire. There's a lot to be done before the sun rises.'

'Us too?' said Daisy hopefully.

'Of course you — Queen Diana, King Aidan,' said Ash.

'We will return you by morning,' said Oak. 'You will have things to set in order before your family come home. The parents, and the bridegroom and the bride.'

'What bridegroom?' asked Dan; and Daisy said, 'Do you mean Margie and Jamie? They're not engaged.'

'I beg your pardon,' said Oak. 'I see I've said what I shouldn't; what the woods hear the house is not to know. Forget it.'

'Not on your life!' said Dan. 'It would be great. I like Jamie.'

'Link hands,' said Oak, grasping Ash with one hand and Larch with the other. 'This is a long journey, no mere trip. All around the bounds of the Forest, and inwards spiralling until we finish at the gathering-floor. Quickly, now, Ash Queen!'

Daisy and Dan linked hands, and Tree joined with Tree all round in twos or little bands. The queen's left hand was held by Oak, but she raised her right arm to the sky. At once a tempestuous rush of air scooped up the whole tree-people — summer and winter, and the two children — into the low cloud and darkness. They were swept away, calling to each other and singing. 'The host of the air,' said Daisy to herself; and Dan thought, 'Better than hang-gliding.' The

169

smells of night air, forest and river, filled their minds and their noses, and all the world became a dizzying rush and swirl.

'We can do this whenever you choose,' shouted Dan to Daisy. 'Queen of the air!'

'Only in winter, fire-king' Daisy yelled back. They laughed until the race of air stopped their mouths, the roar of wind around numbed their senses, and everything went except the glory of the hour.

A note on books and songs

Besides *The Oxford Book of Trees*, the book Daisy and Dan used most for their project was Oliver Rackham's *Trees and Woodland in the British Landscape*.

The human versions of two of the important songs of the tree-people, 'Here we bring new water' and 'Nay, Ivy nay', are in Walter de la Mare's *Come Hither* — the best anthology I know for young people; so is Ben Jonson's 'Hymn to Diana'. 'The Holly and the Ivy', and the May carol, in their human versions, are in *The Oxford Book of Carols*.